MW01122041

MIDNIGHT SUN

Midnight Sun

by
Maja Ardal

Playwrights Canada Press
Toronto•Canada

Midnight Sun © Copyright 2001 Maja Ardal

Playwrights Canada Press
54 Wolseley Street, 2nd Floor
Toronto, Ontario CANADA M5T 1A5
416-703-0201 fax 416-703-0059
info@puc.ca http://www.puc.ca

Playwrights Canada Press acknowledges the support of The Canada Council for the Arts for our publishing programme and the Ontario Arts Council.

Cover photo of Holly Lewis & Paul Braunstein by Cylla Von Tiedemann.
Production Editor: Jodi Armstrong

National Library of Canada Cataloguing in Publication Data

Ardal, Maja
    Midnight sun

A play.
ISBN 0-88754-603-X

I. Title.

PS8551.R74M52   2001   C812'.6   C2001-930201-0
PR9199.3.A72M52   2001

First edition: October 2001
Printed and bound by AGMV Marquis at Quebec, Canada.

*Several attempts were made to obtain permmission to print lyrics from
Hoagy Carmichael and Mitchell Paris song "Stardust" and from the
song "Skylark" by H. Carmichael and J. Mercer. After five months of
delaying publication, pending a reply to our requests, we have gone to
press. Producers of the play should contact Rosemary Gawelko, Warner
Bros. Publications, 15800 N.W. 48th Avenue PO Box 4340,
Miami, Florida 33014. Fax 305-621-1094.*

PLAYWRIGHT ACKNOWLEDGEMENTS

Urjo Kareda and Andrew McKim for inspiration and insight
Harpa and Pall Ardal for stories and memories
Inga Cadranel for revelation
Paul Braunstein for ideas
Also; Gabriel Hogan, Sarah Goggin, Jeff Braunstein

SYNOPSIS

Midnight Sun is situated in Strandvik, a small fictional community in the north of Iceland in 1942, in the days leading up to Midsummer Eve, the time when the sun does not set. Set during the American occupation of Iceland in the Second World War—Iceland was seen as a strategic location for defense—*Midnight Sun*'s subjects are love and country and release.

Most of the play's characters are young Icelanders eager to break out of the limitations of their own tradition: Iceland's hard climate, the long periods of darkness, the tough economy, the remoteness, the narrow range of possibilities. They surrender themselves to the allure of American popular culture. They learn English from Hollywood movies, and the young women style themselves after screen goddesses. They revere, and try to emulate, American music, swing, the blues, the latest crooners' pop-tunes. The seductiveness of a flashy borrowed culture clashes with the Icelanders' mystical response to their own fierce, beautiful landscape, and also with their deep-rooted superstitious beliefs, in which mythological forces are embodied in the "Hiddenfolk," always present but never seen. When American forces actually arrive in the community, the jazzy ease of the US soldiers helps to trigger a sometimes exhilarating, sometimes painful, clash between dreams and reality. *Midnight Sun*'s world of unending light, often tender and liberating, can also cast long, darkening shadows.

SETTING

1942. Strandvik; a small fictional town 40KM south of the Arctic Circle in the North of Iceland. The main industry is fishing, and the town is a market for outlying farms. Strandvik lies a few kilometres from the base of the fiord. Mountains rise behind the town, and on the far side of the fiord. Deeper inland is a flat marsh area leading into a narrowing bordered by sheer cliff-faces. This is Raven Canyon. The rocks around the fiord are formed from lava. This is a treeless environment. At the north end of the fiord, and at its mouth, is the Arctic ocean. Steep cliffs stand sentinel to the open horizon. At night the sun moves in a low circle in the sky from west to east. It will not set until August. The action of this play happens in three days prior to June 21st, Midsummers day.

NOTE

When the Icelandic characters speak to any Americans or speak the names of American screen idols and jazz musicians they speak with an Icelandic accent. The accent is written literally in the "Chattanooga Choo Choo" scene. When Sissa speaks with Clark Gable, she has no accent.

A tape of the Icelandic accent can be made available.
Please contact:

Patricia Ney
Christopher Banks and Associates
6 Adelaide Street East, Suite 610
Toronto, Ontario M5C 1H6
416-214-1155

Midnight Sun was first produced jointly by Tarragon Theatre Main Space, January 23 - February 21, 2001 and National Arts Centre Studio, March 6-17, 2001 with the following cast:

PRILA	Kari Matchett
PETUR	Mathew Edison
KARI	Jeff Madden
HILDUR	Nicky Guadagni
SISSA	Holly Lewis
JIM	Paul Braunstein
SOLDIER/BASSIST	Graig Earle

Co-Directors	Andy McKim & Patricia Vanstone
Music Director	John Roby
Stage Manager	Arwen MacDonell
Asst. Stage Manager	Jason Golinski
Set & Costume Design	Vikki Anderson
Lighting Design	Louise Guinand
Choreographer	Valerie Moore

Songs: "Bad Boy", "Sea Blue Sea" & "We Were Made For Each Other" – Music and lyrics by Maja Ardal.
"Hush My Mamma" – Icelandic Folk Song.

Midnight Sun has been workshopped both at the Tarragon Theatre, and at the Shaw Festival in Niagara-on-the-Lake through the ongoing Shaw-Tarragon co-operative play development program. Thanks to the artists who participated in the several workshop periods: Raoul Bhaneja, Shauna Black, Simon Bradbury, Paul Braunstein, Inga Cadranel, Ben Carlson, Matthew Edison, Patricia Fagan, Kelli Fox, Nicky Guadagni, Patricia Hamilton, Sheri Hollett, Holly Lewis, Kate Lynch, Jeff Madden, Kari Matchett, Andy McKim, Learie McNicolls, Josh Peace, Gordon Rand, Samantha Reynolds, John Roby, Lisa Russell, Tara Samuels, Allan Teichman, Severn Thompson & Patricia Vanstone.

CHARACTERS

PRILA: 21, has lived here all her life. Left school at 16 to help her mother keep house. A wonderful singer. Has been Petur's lover for just over a year. She has raised her youngest sister Sissa since birth. Every Saturday night Prila goes with all the other young people to the local dance at the hotel, dressed as one of the popular Hollywood stars of the the day. She speaks a little English, learned from watching Hollywood films. She has just got the job of the town telephone operator. She is thought of as the "prettiest girl in town."

SISSA: 13. She will have a fourteenth birthday in 3 days. Prila's younger sister, the youngest in the family. Sissa prefers the imaginary world to reality. She is always play-acting characters from Hollywood films, and has been known to wander around the house at night in her sleep. Her mother gave birth to her the night her husband died, and has always seen her as the extra child she did not want.

HILDUR: Late 40s. Widow. Prila and Sissa's mother. Her husband died suddenly, leaving her with debts and no pension from his job. She lives in a big house above the town on top of a cliff. She has five sons ranging in age from 18 to 30. They are at sea, working on fishing trawlers, and shipping the cod and herring catch to Britain. They do not send money home. She does not have any guests in the house except Petur. She dislikes the townspeople, and has no respect for religion. She has been a widow for 14 years. She has the same healthy respect for the Hiddenfolk as most Icelanders have.

PETUR: 21. Kari's younger half-brother. Lives in the home of a wealthy old aunt. His mother died when he was 10, and his father was a well-known poet. Petur was the top scholar in High School, achieving the coveted scholarship to study abroad. Petur is respected in the town, and speaks fine English. Prila was his childhood chum, and now they are lovers.

KARI: 23. Petur's half-brother. They had the same mother. Kari's father, still alive, is a deadbeat drunk on his last legs. Kari is a gifted musician. Well-known in this part of Iceland for his great piano playing at the dances. His Aunt supported his musical studies in Copenhagen, where he played jazz piano, and recently discovered the cornet. Was Prila's lover until departing for Copenhagen. Kari was the most socially popular young man in town before he left. However his blackout drinking bouts escalated during his youth, and he became the most violent fighter at the weekend dances.

PRIVATE JIM BAILEY (Jim Swing): 23. Newly-arrived American air force soldier. From Kansas. He is stationed in Raven Canyon Air base. Hosts the newly set up army radio station. Is a talented drummer.

NOTES ON CASTING

KARI: The role calls for skill playing piano and rudimentary skill in cornet/trumpet, as well as singing. However this role has been successfully portrayed by an actor with only the singing and dramatic skills. Recorded piano and cornet can be played when necessary. The most important element in casting is the dramatic.

JIM: In this text Jim plays drums. This was written after an actor/drummer was cast. Jim can play any instrument suitable for jazz, and *the playwright should be contacted to adjust the text accordingly.*

NOTES ON SHEET-PULLING

The characters take a sheet, and, holding a corner in each hand, stand opposite one another. They pull the sheet leaning away from each other, and after each pull, they gather a fist full of sheet, continuing until they have gathered the sheet together. They then open up the sheet again and start to fold it. First long ways, then towards one another. The pulling is a rhythmic motion, and the fun in the scene is that Hildur pulls harder than Sissa, pulling her almost off her feet at times.

ABOUT THE HIDDENFOLK

Icelanders have a rich folkloric world. Supernatural beings populate the landscape, and the ones which are unique to Iceland are Huldufolk. In English this translates to Hiddenfolk. These characters are human-sized and live in the mountain cliffs. History tells us that they should be left alone to pursue their lives alongside humans. Even today, in modern Iceland, there is respect for the Hiddenfolk. During the 1950s, when a road was being built across their homes, the machinery broke down, and the road had to be re-routed. Children are most likely to be able to see them, especially highly sensitive children like SISSA.

ACT ONE

Saturday Night.

*As the lights fade slowly down in the house, the stage
area becomes filled with a smoky haze. Sounds of hundreds of male voices in a huge hall. The intro to the
song starts instrumentally. There is no colour on the
stage. It is like a black and white movie. As the lights
come completely down, shadows appear against the
back wall. A drummer, the shadow long and distorted
right to the ceiling, his hands pounding the drum and
high hat. A stand-up bassist plucks the strings, head
bent over the swaying instrument. The profile of a
cornet player lifts his head to the heavens, and when
we hear the first note of the woman's voice, a slinky,
wide-shouldered female shadow, hair done up Rita
Hayworth style, leans in on the centre of the action
in front of a microphone. Her body is moving
rhythmically to the beat, and the sound of men's
voices subsides as the song takes over. It is PRILA
in her Rita Hayworth dress.*

PRILA   (*singing*) "What good is melody what good is music
If it ain't possessin' something sweet?
It ain't the melody it ain't the music
There's something else that makes the tune complete
It don't mean a thing if it ain't got that swing
Doo wah do wah do wah do wah do wah do wah do
wah
It don't mean a thing all you gotta do is sing
Doo wah...
It makes no difference if it's sweet or hot
just give that rhythm everything you've got"

    *The back wall begins to glow red. A small figure –
SISSA, floats, candle in hand, into a recess of the stage
area. The cellar of the house. She is wearing a dress
which looks like Dorothy's in the "Wizard of Oz."*

"Oh it don't mean a thing if it ain't got that swing
Doo wah..."

*Song starts to sound hollow and distant. SISSA
dances and starts to speak over the last "Do wa's."
What we see is now in colour. The back wall is
now completely red. We hear the sound of people
whispering – almost singing. SISSA is in the presence
of the Hiddenfolk. She has the gift of being able to
see them. For those of us who cannot, they are
human-sized, and live a parallel life to humans. They
live inside the rocky ridges and cliffs of the mountains.*

SISSA   (*speaking to someone unseen under the floor of the cellar*)
They're here! Sssh! Sssh! You don't have to cry any
more. Your family all came back. (*She gestures to the
Hiddenfolk and the sound of whispery voices swells up.*)
Come closer Hiddenfolk! (*to girl in the rock*) They've
come to take you to your new home across the fiord.
(*She speaks to the Hiddenfolk whom she sees standing
around her.*) Oh, yes! I hear your little girl crying. (*to
invisible girl*) But you're NOT a baby any more, are
you! You were born just before this house was built,
and you're already fourteen! Oh I wish you could talk
to me. When I'm confirmed in three days time, I will
ask God to forgive my father for what he did. We'll
all pray for the rock to break open, and you will come
out, all ready for your confirmation, and you'll be a
woman too!

*The Whispers becomes mournful, turning to the sound
of the wind whistling. A bluster of rain rattles the
tiny cellar window.*

SISSA   (*calling upstairs*) Mamma! (*She leaves the cellar.*)

Wednesday.

*We are in the large kitchen of HILDUR's house.
Morning. Outside it is grey and drizzly. At one end
of the kitchen is a telephone exchange covered with a
cloth. In the middle of the room is the area for eating.
A dress is draped over a chair. It is PRILA's unfinished
dress for the dance. Out of sight is the area for cooking.*

HILDUR (*coming in from outside with a huge armload of dry laundry*) Sissa! The rain's started again. You could have helped me bring this in.

SISSA (*enters kitchen*) "Come out come out wherever you are, And see the young lady who fell from a star."

HILDUR If you could sing like your big sister I wouldn't mind, but that's just tuneless noise. (*calls*) Prila! Get up before that thing begins to ring!

SISSA "She fell from a star, she fell very far..."

HILDUR (*to PRILA, off*) I've been awake all night with all the noise of that telephone exchange being set up, and now I've overslept. The day's half over!

SISSA (*pulls cover off the exchange*) Telephone exchange!

HILDUR *Don't touch it!* As for you! Up and down, up and down the hallway all night long. I hope you were awake this time. You could fall down stairs, then we'll find you dead in the morning with a broken neck!

SISSA Mamma, you probably forgot I'm turning 14 on Friday. I want to have the confirmation ceremony right here. Pastor Jon said he'd do it, but I have to ask you first.

HILDUR I haven't had any guests in this house for fourteen years. I'm not going to start now. Where's your sister? (*calling*) Prila!

SISSA *And* – I want a real name. Prila got one.

HILDUR Sissa. It's good enough.

SISSA Little sister?!

HILDUR Prila called you Sissa. Now it's stuck.

SISSA I want to be christened on my birthday too. I want to wear white, and have Pastor Jon pour holy water on my head.

HILDUR   No religious ceremony in this house!

SISSA   You had a funeral. That's a religious ceremony

HILDUR   The funeral was necessary. Christening you wasn't. And they forced it on me because your father was so important.

SISSA   So am I!

HILDUR   You won't be any better for having Pastor Jon christen you.

SISSA   And confirm me!

HILDUR   No confirmation either! Get the coffee.

SISSA   No!

HILDUR   Prila!

> *PRILA hurries in excitedly. She goes to the telephone exchange, picks up the headphones and examines the switches.*

PRILA   Don't bother me. I overslept!

HILDUR   The telephone exchange in my house! Who would have dreamed!

PRILA   Did it ring yet?

HILDUR   It'll never stop when this town finds out you're the new operator.

PRILA   Mamma is the coffee ready?

HILDUR   So now I have to do everything? (*leaves*)

SISSA   Prila! The Hiddenfolk are back for my confirmation!

PRILA   (*shocked*) Did you see them?

SISSA	Yes. In the cellar. They're staying till I turn fourteen.
PRILA	(*trying to concentrate on the switchboard*) What?! They're going to be down there for three days?
SISSA	And after the ceremony, their little girl will be set free.
PRILA	(*The exchange buzzes.*) Oh! Ah – How do I–
SISSA	(*continues over PRILA's panic*) The one that got left behind when she was a baby.
PRILA	Shut up!– (*on line*) –Oh sorry, not you. This is the Northern Iceland telephone exchange. Skipper Lalli! Yes it's Prila. Thank you. I'll put you through– (*does it*)
SISSA	It's just like you always told me. And it's all coming true.
PRILA	The Hiddenfolk can't have come here because of a baby!
SISSA	Why not?
PRILA	There has to be another reason.
SISSA	My confirmation!
PRILA	How on earth will you persuade Mamma to give you a confirmation, you dreamer! Oh God! They'd better stay hidden from her. After fourteen years – she'll think it's an omen.
SISSA	She can't see the Hiddenfolk. They told me. They'll leave again after my birthday. With their little girl.
PRILA	Just make sure they do–
SISSA	And I'll build them little houses, and a brick road. I'll come over the rainbow to visit them and turn it all to colour!

PRILA   Those munchkins in the "Wizard of Oz" aren't real!!
         You can't compare them to the Hiddenfolk! Now get
         lost! I can't afford to lose this job!

SISSA   Call me Dorothy.

PRILA   Dorothy? It's an improvement on Scarlett.

SISSA   (*in an Icelandic accent*) Frankly my dear, I don't give a
         damn!

         Telephone buzzes.

PRILA   Northern Iceland telephone! Putting you through.

         *HILDUR comes in with coffee and mugs. SISSA grabs
         a cup and spoons lots of sugar into it.*

SISSA   Mamma! I have the Hiddenfolk in the cellar.

HILDUR   (*startled*) *What*? You've seen them?!

PRILA   She's just been in the red currant wine, Mamma.

HILDUR   Prila, she's just to have one cup at bedtime. And keep
         the cellar door locked from now on. Sissa's not to go
         down there!

SISSA   No! You can't do that! I was probably just dreaming.

PRILA   She's Dorothy today.

HILDUR   Well Dorothy should keep her dreams to herself.

SISSA   Mamma.

HILDUR   (*grabbing the sugar bowl from SISSA*) That's enough!
         You know it's rationed!

SISSA   Mamma, do I look like Judy Garland?

HILDUR   Never heard of her.

SISSA   She's a film star and she's beautiful.

HILDUR   No. Help me pull the sheets.

                The sheet pulling continues as PRILA speaks on the phone.

PRILA   Svana! It's Prila! I got the operator job! Much better than the dairy. And this job pays in cash! I'll treat you to the Bio [*Beeoh*] next week.

HILDUR   After you've paid for your keep.

SISSA   I'm coming to the Bio! They're showing Judy Garland and Gene Kelly in "Me and My Gal."

PRILA   (*on phone*) Have you finished sewing your dress for the Midsummer Dance on Saturday?

SISSA   (*pulling the sheet dreamily*) My first Midsummer Dance!

HILDUR   Come on, girl! (*yanks her end of the sheet*) Pull!

PRILA   Oh you'll look great as Katherine Hepburn. That dress in "Philadelphia Story!"

SISSA   The white dress with the sequins! It's *so* beautiful!

PRILA   I'm going to be Rita Hayworth.

                SISSA drops the sheet and grabs PRILA's dance dress.

SISSA   This one? (*holds it in front of herself*)

PRILA   (*to SISSA*) Leave it!

HILDUR   Get *back* here!

PRILA   Wasn't that awful last year, when Helena from the Hot Spring was in the Ginger Rogers dress just like yours!

SISSA   I'm going to fall in love at the dance.

HILDUR   Who's the lucky boy?

PRILA   Are you still going to let Ingi take you? (*listens to Svana*)

SISSA   Lucky Man! I'll be a *woman* on Saturday.

PRILA   Just like all the guys. Too proud to say he loves you, even when he's full of liquor! Give him up.

HILDUR   Pull harder! (*She yanks at the sheet pulling SISSA nearly off her feet.*)

> PETUR enters. He goes straight to PRILA who doesn't see him, and kisses her neck.

PRILA   Petur!

SISSA   (*Delighted, she drops the sheet.*) Petur!

PRILA   (*to Svana*) I'll call you back.

PETUR   Prila Switchboard! Looks good on you. (*PRILA laughs.*) I couldn't get through to you on the phone. Come here. (*grabs her hand*)

PRILA   I've got to work–

HILDUR   Petur Professor! The coffee's hot.

PETUR   No time, Hildur. Look out the window! Ships horns. There's a fleet just entering the fiord! Americanis! They've picked us!

PRILA   (*looks*) Oh my God! That's the biggest ship I've ever seen!

PETUR   It's a battleship. See the flags?

HILDUR   What? (*runs to the window*)

SISSA   Let me see! Let me see!

HILDUR   What the hell is that? It's filled up the whole Harbour!

SISSA   (*pushes past them to look*) Oh! Oh! Oh! They're here!

PETUR   The Americani air forces have been scouting around for the perfect northern base, and they've picked us.

PRILA   They've chosen Strandvik?

HILDUR   It's a monster!

PETUR   They're setting up a big air base in Raven Canyon.

                        Drone of Bombers overhead.

HILDUR   (*sees Bombers*) They've brought the war! The next thing, we'll see Germans bombing the fiord–

PETUR   Not with the Americanis here. They're setting up anti-aircraft guns all over the mountain ridges.

SISSA   The Hiddenfolk ridge? Oh no! They're going to get angry.

PETUR   Don't talk about Hiddenfolk stuff to the Americanis. They'll think we're pagans.

HILDUR   So what?

PRILA   The whole fiord's full of boats!

PETUR   100 Icelandic trawlers from the south. Full of Americani soldiers.

PRILA   How many Americanis?

PETUR   Two thousand!

PRILA   (*laughs*) That's twice the male population!

PETUR   And Olaf the Mayor came by my house, to ask *me* to give the welcome speech!

PRILA   Why?

PETUR   He can't speak English. Hildur! Come down for the celebrations!

HILDUR   I'm not going to welcome any army!

PETUR   I have to run! (*leaves*)

SISSA   Lipstick, lipstick! Lipstick! (*rummages around in PRILA's pockets, and in the little purse beside PRILA's chair*)

PRILA   (*at telephone exchange*) Hallo! Everyone who's listening in! The Americani soldiers are here! Two thousand men! (*to SISSA*) Leave that alone! It's expensive! (*She grabs the lipstick from SISSA and puts it on. She grabs a pair of shoes.*) Come on, Mamma!

HILDUR   I'm not going anywhere!

PRILA   Yes you are! This is the biggest thing that's happened since father died! Come on!

HILDUR   Well wait for me! I'm not going down there alone! Prila! (*PRILA runs out. HILDUR follows.*) I'm just going down to hear the professor speak. That's all!

PRILA   He's not a professor yet, Mamma.

SISSA   At last! My Hollywood saviour comes to the rescue!

> *She runs outside in gum boots with lipstick smeared on her lips and cheeks. She looks like a deranged Dorothy. Ships' horns are blowing, planes are flying overhead. A band is playing a military American brass tune through speakers. Ocean birds are screaming. SISSA is up high on a rock, waving to the sky.*

Hallo Americanis!

> *An American soldier arrives. He is wearing bullets crossed over his chest. He looks identical to Clark Gable. On his arrival a bright sun streams out from the clouds.*

SOLDIER Hi, Sis!

SISSA You know my name!

SOLDIER Sure do, little sister. You speak American!

SISSA (*without an Icelandic accent*) You speak Icelandic!

SOLDIER I speak whatever you do.

SISSA You brought the sun.

SOLDIER I always do.

SISSA You are my angel.

SOLDIER And you sure are a cute little Icelander.

The Harbour.

PETUR steps up to a microphone. SISSA and the soldier are in a dreamland of their own.

PETUR (*in accented but quite good English*) Good day! I am representative Petur Karlsson. The town of Strandvik receives you with an open arm! And a shining sun. The first sunshine we have seen in a month. We congratulate you and your great country for finally joining the battle to punish the fascist. Perhaps with your fine army Hitler will be defeated before the end of 1942! You will see that Icelanders are a friendly and graceful people. Now we are happy to play for you the Anthem of our country, sung by the National Choir of Iceland!

The anthem rises up above the other sounds. KARI appears at the harbour carrying a small cornet case. He stands and listens, unseen by the others. The anthem fades to background.

SISSA (*mimicking the Munchkins and waving the Icelandic flag*) "As mayor of the munchkin city In the country of the land of Oz

We welcome you most regally–
but we have to verify it legally."

SOLDIER Well, thanks, little munchkin!

SISSA (*sighs adoringly*) Oh Clark Gable!

SOLDIER You know me in this disguise?

SISSA I saw "Gone with the Wind." You are the most handsome Americani in the world!

SOLDIER You're a fan.

SISSA And you really *are* in colour! When I was being Scarlett I never stopped loving you!

SOLDIER And that's the way it was *meant* to be.

> *"Cheek to Cheek" swells up, as the anthem fades into an echoey background.*

SISSA Suddenly I feel like dancing.

SOLDIER (*bows, takes her hand and kisses it*) May I have the honour?

SISSA I have no shoes.

> *Two ruby slippers appear magically, or out of his pockets. He gives them to her. SISSA takes off her boots and puts them on, clicks her heels.*

There's no place like Hollywood, there's no place like Hollywood!

> *They dance.*

> *KARI goes to his parlour. He plays along with "Cheek to Cheek" on the cornet. HILDUR, in the kitchen, starts to make cookies. PRILA sits at the exchange.*

3PM **Wednesday. Kari and Petur's Parlour.**

PETUR enters from the harbour with his camera and notebook.

PETUR What the hell – Kari! Am I seeing a ghost?
       KARI stops playing.

KARI   Well, look at you little brother! A whole head taller, and a lot better looking! (*embraces PETUR*)

PETUR (*pushes him back*) You stink of diesel fumes and–

KARI   Ah yes. I forgot I'm in the civilized clutches of Aunt Anna's palace. Aren't you glad to see me?

PETUR Uh – of course – I'm just trying to get over the shock. Two years, and suddenly.... What's this? (*indicates cornet*)

KARI   My new love.

PETUR What happened to the piano?

KARI   A piano you love makes you want to stay. With this, I make music wherever I go.

PETUR How did you get here? I thought it was impossible to get out of Denmark.

KARI   Nothing's impossible. You know me. Three weeks on a trawler dodging mines and U-boats. But I've still got my fingers and my lips. Run and find Prila for me.

PETUR Prila? I don't think–

KARI   I've got a singing job for her with the Americani band. There's a whole new world here. Music heaven. Good time to come back. (*beat*) That was a poetic speech. You are your father's son.

PETUR Your father was there.

KARI   He's not dead yet?

PETUR   He was half-way through a bottle of Americani whisky.

KARI   His lucky day.

PETUR   You should have written.

KARI   D'you think it's easy getting mail out of Denmark?

PETUR   You could have let us know where you were living. I might have kept you up with news.

KARI   So tell me. Have you finally discovered love?

PETUR   Yes, actually.

KARI   Who? Is she beautiful?

PETUR   Very. I'll surprise you. (*changing subject*) I have a job reporting for the *Morning News*.

KARI   And you've graduated of course?

PETUR   Top scholar. I'm off to university in Boston in September.

KARI   Where's our aunt?

PETUR   Gone to visit the homestead in Troll's Tongue.

KARI   Good! I can play all night. (*plays a classical piece*)

PETUR   So? Did Aunt Anna succeed in turning you into a concert pianist?

KARI   (*laughs*) No. (*makes the classical piece sound jazzy*)

PETUR   If you didn't spend her money at the Academy she deserves to be told.

KARI   She doesn't own me. If I choose to play jazz in clubs instead of Mozart for matrons, that's my business.

PETUR   And now you're back sitting in front of her piano.

KARI   My piano.

PETUR   What makes it yours?

KARI   The way I handle it. (*plays something tender and lyrical*)

PETUR   If you only handled people the same.

KARI   Your big brother is back. A welcome would have been nice.

PETUR   What do you want? The red carpet?

KARI   Sure. Why not?

PETUR   And by the way, Prila's lost interest in singing.

KARI   (*plays and sings*) "We were made for each other, I for you, you for me,"

PETUR   Just don't come back and make me clean up your mess again.

KARI   "Two parts of one heart my sweetheart together eternally..."

PETUR   (*pulls a wad of bills out of his pocket*) Same old Kari. This'll keep you going. (*puts it on the piano and leaves*)

KARI   (*takes the money and puts it in his pocket*) Same old Kari. (*plays a fast jazzy lick on the piano*)

10 o'clock Wednesday. Hildur's house.

> *Kitchen. HILDUR has a tray of cookies for the oven. She goes off to put them in.*

PRILA   (*at telephone exchange*) Closing down Strandvik exchange, 'till 7 o'clock tomorrow. All you gossips listening – Goodnight!

> *PRILA opens a pack of gum, pops a piece into her mouth, and picks up her dress. Holds it up and looks at it.*

Finally! Some excitement in Strandvik! And jobs.

HILDUR   (*from off*) I saw the local men getting cash just for signing onto the work crews.

PRILA   Nothing like a pocketful of money.

HILDUR   (*coming in*) I don't trust it. I'd sooner trade my knitting and eggs for wool and–

PRILA   (*cutting her off*) Those days are dead and gone. Do you want to be dirt poor all your life? It's a new world, old woman.

HILDUR   Your brothers could have used that kind of job instead of going out on the sea in the middle of a war.

PRILA   You were glad to get those thugs off your hands, Mamma. They'd have drunk it all away whether they're working for the Americanis or shipping fish to Britain.

HILDUR   Why couldn't I have had a son like the professor?

PRILA   Don't start on that.

HILDUR   Is that your dress for the dance?

PRILA   Exact copy of Rita Hayworth's.

HILDUR   Who?

PRILA   Finish the hem off for me while I do the neckline.

HILDUR   This is *short*.

PRILA   Just at the knees.

HILDUR   At the *knees*? You'll need nice stockings then.

PRILA   I can just draw a line. (*indicates the back of her leg*)

HILDUR   It looks stupid.

PRILA   Well, I don't *have* any stockings!

           They settle down to sew.

HILDUR   I saw Big Didda from the dairy getting a pair of
           stockings. She kissed an Americani. Slut.

PRILA   Well I'm not going to make some Americani happy
           by taking his presents.

HILDUR   You already have. You look like a sheep chewing
           grass.

PRILA   (*opens a pack of gum*) Chewing gum! Come on,
           Mamma, try some!

HILDUR   I don't want to look like a sheep!

PRILA   You already are! This one tastes like oranges. (*reads the
           Juicy Fruit label*) Dzoossy froott.

HILDUR   (*tempted*) I'll take a tiny piece. (*takes it and chews as if
           she's eating poison*)

PRILA   Don't swallow it.

HILDUR   Then what's the point?

PRILA   Does there have to be one?

HILDUR   What will they invent next! (*chews with difficulty*) Why
           do Americanis smile all the time?

PRILA   They're rich.

HILDUR   They look simple.

PRILA   It's good to see some smiling around this town.

HILDUR   When do I spit it out?

PRILA   Not yet!

HILDUR   Where's your sister?

PRILA   I'm not watching her any more.

HILDUR   Then who will?

PRILA   You'd better get ready Mamma, I'm leaving soon.

HILDUR   Why? Where to?

PRILA   Who knows? You don't expect me to stay in this town all my life, seeing my whole future laid out in front of me?

HILDUR   You can't leave me alone with her. I can't control her.

PRILA   You never bothered to learn.

HILDUR   She's missed all her chores.

PRILA   She's probably running around with the soldiers.

HILDUR   She'd better not be.

PRILA   If you weren't so busy hiding from Sigga Psychic and her gang of gossips you could have followed her.

HILDUR   I was listening to the professor's speech. That Petur Karlsson's a clever boy. I didn't understand a word he said.

PRILA   Didn't you hear Old Ulla? "There's Hildur the Horrible's half-wit daughter."

HILDUR   You're the one who makes her into an idiot, teaching her about those film stars as if it's real life.

PRILA   What's wrong with a little romance?

HILDUR   You'd better tell her about sex now that those soldier boys are here. Doesn't take much to get a name in this town.

PRILA   You should know. (*a momentary chill between the women*) She's trying to follow me and Petur to bed now.

HILDUR   That's one way to learn.

PRILA   She's got it in her head that the Hiddenfolk won't leave the house till she's confirmed.

HILDUR   So they *are* here! I should have known.

PRILA   You should go along with Sissa just in case they *do* cause trouble. You've ignored her birthday since she was born.

HILDUR   I'm not inviting hordes of people into this house.

PRILA   People forget.

HILDUR   I don't!

PRILA   It's been 14 years since the funeral–

HILDUR   They didn't come to pay their respects to the corpse of Haraldur. They came to see my misery. (*laughs*) They'll never get the satisfaction.

PRILA   (*chanting the taunt she has heard all her life*) "Crazy Hildur never goes to pray, spat on the bible and the priest ran away!" (*beat*) I was there too, Mamma!

HILDUR   You've turned out just fine.

PRILA   She's unhappy.

HILDUR   Most people are miserable. That's just life.

PRILA   Aaargh! You're an old troll!

HILDUR   Exactly! And you know what happens to trolls when they get caught by the sunrise.

PRILA   Yes! But you're *already* a big lump of rock!

> *SISSA enters carrying a carton of cigarettes, chewing gum. She is drunk.*

SISSA   (*singing*) "I'm in heaven" – la da da da–

PRILA   Where have you been?

SISSA   Dancing with Clark Gable.

PRILA   You'll get a name.

SISSA   Good because I don't have one.

HILDUR   You want to be called soldier slut?

SISSA   He will *never* call me that. He's my Americani
              saviour.

PRILA   What is he saving you from?

SISSA   Life!

PRILA   The soldiers have a bigger job than rescuing you.

SISSA   My soldier doesn't. He says when I become a woman,
              he'll fly me over the rainbow and into Hollywood!
              We'll drink *cocks tails* with a cherry and laugh and
              kiss and my lipstick will never come off!

PRILA   When did *you* learn to speak English?

HILDUR   If you girls are going to spend so much time
              swooning over soldiers, you might as well keep
              idle fingers busy. Where's your knitting?

PRILA   I'm not knitting any more. (*pulls socks out of her pocket*)
              I bought these from old Soffia.

HILDUR   Next thing you'll see a hole in the heel and throw
              them out!

PRILA   Maybe I will.

HILDUR   Knitting kept this country alive. (*The girls join in,
              mimicking their mother.*) "The sheep is the Icelander's
              best friend! Loyal, through good times and bad."
              (*HILDUR glares at them. They stop and giggle.*) When
              the war is over, times will be bad again. It's a cycle.
              Agh! I swallowed it! (*She gags. The girls laugh.*) No
              respect. You'd better drink some coffee, Dorothy.

SISSA   Sissa!

HILDUR   Oh, now we're back to Sissa?

SISSA   He said "Hi Sis."

PRILA   They call all women that. You're drunk.

SISSA   I'm *happy*!

HILDUR   (*to PRILA*) See? She *is* happy. I'll put on the water. (*exits*)

> *PRILA brushes SISSA's hair, and wipes the lipstick off her face.*

PRILA   Have you been drinking with the soldiers?

SISSA   Clark Gable gave me liquor. It's much better than the red currant wine.

PRILA   And much stronger. Don't let them pour that poison into you. And you're only to drink the wine in the cellar at bedtime.

SISSA   It gives me good dreams all day.

PRILA   There's a difference between dreaming and waking.

SISSA   What is it?

PRILA   Feel this? (*pulls her hair hard*)

SISSA   Oww! That hurt!

PRILA   You're awake.

SISSA   That wine in the cellar's holy blood. I need to drink it for my confirmation.

PRILA   I'm trying to help you get confirmed, idiot! Just behave yourself until your birthday, or I *will* lock the cellar door!

PETUR arrives.

PETUR   How was I, Prila? Did I make a fool of myself?

PRILA   You were like Jimmy Stewart in "Mr. Smith goes to Washington."

PETUR   (*pleased*) Really?

SISSA   (*in raptures*) Jimmy Stewart!

HILDUR   (*comes in*) Petur! That was a very impressive speech. I've got sugar biscuits in the oven for you.

PETUR   Thank you, Hildur. Coming to the Midsummer Dance on Saturday?

HILDUR   Do I have to look like Rita Haystack?

PETUR   You should wear your traditional dress.

HILDUR   I haven't worn that for fourteen years, maybe I should.

PRILA   Mamma go and get the biscuits.

HILDUR leaves laughing.

Are you inviting her to the dance, or me?

PETUR   I won't go without you. You make me look like Gene Kelly when we dance.

PRILA   Glad to be of service.

SISSA   Hey, sis! Gotta light?

PETUR   No. I'll take these. (*He takes the cigarettes.*)

SISSA   No! They're mine!

PETUR   Leave us. Prila and I have to talk.

PRILA   We do?

SISSA   What about?

PETUR   None of your business.

>*An airplane flies overhead.*

SISSA   An airplane! More soldiers!

>*They dash out to look.*

HILDUR   (*rushes out after them*) What the hell's going on? (*Speakers blare "Sing Sing Sing."*) What now? (*They stand outside and look up as paper leaflets flutter all around them like snow.*) We're being bombed!

>*They pick the leaflets up as the plane flies off. Music fades to a distance.*

SISSA   What does it say?

PETUR   (*reads*) The Americanis are holding a dance this Saturday. At The Temperance Hall.

HILDUR   Ha ha! They work fast. (*She goes back inside.*)

PETUR   (*reading the flyer*) "Big Band Bash! Ladies of Strandvik, come and meet the new guys in town."

PRILA   Only Ladies?

PETUR   That's just the way they talk. I'm sure they mean everyone.

PRILA   What else does it say?

PETUR   Free drinks all night.

PRILA   Free drinks for Strandvik men on a Saturday night? They'll regret it.

SISSA   In the Temperance Hall!

PETUR   But we've got the Midsummer Dance at the Hotel on Saturday.

PRILA   Why don't we all just go to their Big-Band-Bash?

SISSA   I'm going!

PETUR   That's a lot of planning up in smoke. Moving 500
          men and women over to the Americani dance. I'd
          have to convince my committee.

PRILA   You *are* the committee.

SISSA   I'm going as Bette Davis in "Dark Victory." I'll have a
          brain tumour and I'll get drunk and the doctor will
          fall in love with me–

PRILA   (*ignoring her and speaking to PETUR*) I'll do you up as
          Jimmy Stewart in "Philadelphia Story." (*speaking as
          Katherine*) "Put me in your pocket Mike." (*fakes a
          swoon into his arms*)

PETUR   (*at a loss*) What do I say?

SISSA   Just kiss her like Jimmy Stewart did!

PRILA   (*stands up*) We'll show the Americanis we're not some
          old world sod-hut-dwellers.

PETUR   I don't know. It'd be fun to arrive by horse.

PRILA   My Rita Hayworth dress won't fit over the back of a
          horse.

PETUR   The sight of your hair flying in the wind, and a slinky
          dress stretched over a horse's backside will make the
          whole town crazy! And the Americanis very jealous.
          I can see the colours of the sky in your eyes.

PRILA   My eyes are red?

PETUR   No – I uh – well, I'm not that good at compliments.

SISSA   You should have said, "Darling, the sky has sparked a
          fire of passion in your lovely eyeballs," then–

PETUR   (*cuts SISSA off*) Prila–

PRILA	Yes?
PETUR	I – ah–
SISSA	Yes?
PETUR	I – I still don't quite believe what's happened to us.
PRILA	(*teasingly*) I do. How long do *you* need?
PETUR	Tell me – do you ever miss–
PRILA	Kari? (*laughs*) Why would you even think to ask?
PETUR	Kari? I – wasn't thinking of him. I meant singing.
PRILA	Oh. Singing. Yes. I dream about it sometimes.
PETUR	You do?
PRILA	In some smoky bar in Chicago. Singing "Skylark" with Hoagy Carmichael.
PETUR	Oh.
PRILA	It's just a dream.
PETUR	I've got one.
PRILA	Tell me.
PETUR	It's about you. And me.
PRILA	Go on...
PETUR	I – romantic language – it's not my style–
SISSA	Try saying it like Clark Gable, Petur, that might help.
PRILA	Sissa!
SISSA	Too scared! You'll never be like Clark Gable. (*She wanders off a little way and watches.*)

PETUR   (*getting the courage*) Well, now that I have the
         scholarship to study in Boston, I want to – bring
         you with me.

         He waits. Pause.

PRILA   I wondered if you were going to ask me.

PETUR   I've wanted to for a year, but I wasn't sure if you
         were – over – I mean completely.

PRILA   Recovered? Take my pulse, doctor.

         PETUR takes her wrist. She smiles.

         You do that to me. Now make me a promise.

PETUR   Anything.

PRILA   Promise never to make me talk about the past.

PETUR   I promise.

PRILA   Now ask me.

PETUR   Ask you? I thought we – I thought I just did–

PRILA   Oh no!

PETUR   Um... (*looks at the sky and says formally*) Will you be my
         wife?

SISSA   You certainly botched that up! Say "I love you!"

PRILA   Do you think you could say it again and look at me
         this time?

PETUR   No.

SISSA   (*lighting two cigarettes for PRILA and PETUR who take
         them without acknowledging her*) Bette Davis gazes at
         her lover. The smoke from their cigarettes blends in a
         sensuous dance of love. He says, "Will you be happy,
         Charlotte?" "Oh, Gerry," says Bette, "Don't let's ask
         for the moon! We have the stars!"

PETUR   This is not a film, Sissa!

SISSA   Now's your chance! Throw her on the ground! Make mad passionate love under the stars! The sun!

PRILA   (*as Garbo*) "Vee vant to be alone!"

PETUR   You haven't answered me.

            KARI appears.

SISSA   Kari! (*runs into his arms*) Kari Jazzplayer!

KARI   Hallo, Prila. (*He gazes at her.*) God! You're more beautiful than ever.

SISSA   Oh it's like a movie! You've arrived just in time to play at the ceremony! (*suddenly practical*) You can play something romantic on the piano and sing love songs, while Petur slips the wedding ring upon her finger! They're going to be *married*!

            Shocked silence.

KARI   (*to PRILA*) Is this true? (*to PETUR*) So this is the kind of surprise you had in mind for me. A punch-in-the-face surprise. You shit!

PETUR   You have no–!

PRILA   (*interrupting*) Petur!

KARI   Prila – are you...? (*She doesn't answer.*) Alright. Sorry I interrupted the uh – mood. (*He goes.*)

SISSA   "Toto, I have a feeling we're not in Kansas any more!"

            KARI goes back and sits at the piano in his parlour.

HILDUR   (*comes out with a cup of coffee and a small plate of sweet biscuits for PETUR*) What was Sissa yelling about? Oh! Professor. Here.

SISSA   Sugar biscuits! (*grabs for one*)

HILDUR   They're just for him! (*She hands PETUR the plate. He holds the plate and doesn't eat them. SISSA proceeds to eat them all off the plate.*) You know, professor, with these handsome uniforms in town, you'd better move fast, before she gets snatched up by a soldier. They're on the hunt, and she's a lovely girl. Grab her now! Propose!

PETUR   Prila–?

PRILA   (*to PETUR*) You knew he was back.

HILDUR   (*oblivious, breathes deep and looks at the sky*) You can smell the sex in this town.

PETUR   (*to PRILA*) Yes.

HILDUR   And it's not just the usual bulls and rams in heat. There's a new smell. Cigarettes, cologne, and male sweat. Keep her close. Hang on tight!

PETUR   Will you–?

HILDUR   That damned sun. It boils the blood. (*She sticks two sugar lumps behind her teeth and slurps her coffee loudly.*)

PRILA   You'll have to ask me again.

PETUR   Because he's back?

PRILA   Because you chose the wrong time.

          They stand on the hillside looking out at the midnight sun.

Raven Canyon Radio Station Midnight Wednesday

          We hear it on the army base speakers.

JIM   (*on radio*) Midnight at the edge of the world. This is Raven Canyon Radio-voice of the USA. The first American troop broadcast from latitude 66 North. I am Private Jim Bailey filling in for Sergeant Cooper who's still out on the icy waves hunting down

U-boats. Good luck Sarge and thanks for the job. This is a heap better than chasing wolf packs in a hurricane. I'll be keeping you all up-to-date, with daily reports from the 20 thousand Americans stationed all around the coast of Iceland. So unpack your gear boys, and dream about those Northern dames! Gee, just when we thought we'd go blind looking for the enemy in gale force winds, a beauty pageant welcomes us at the harbour. Now let's open up the airwaves and give this cool little town something BIG and HOT! (*puts on a record*) I am your host, Jim Swing!

> *Spins "In the Mood." Loudspeakers blare. JIM dances. PRILA and PETUR start to dance. They swing around getting in HILDUR's way. SISSA dances alone. KARI sits at the piano.*

Morning Thursday. Kari's house.

SISSA   (*enters*) Kari Jazzplayer. You were in my dream.

KARI   I'm glad I'm in somebody's.

SISSA   The king of the humans had built a huge castle for his queen on the Hiddenfolk Cliff. It looked like the Emerald City. But the little baby girl was trapped under the castle inside the rock. Hundreds of Hiddenfolk came back crying for their baby. But the rock wouldn't open. They were so angry they choked the king to death and put a rock in the queen's heart. Then all at once there was the most beautiful music, like the trumpeting of angels, and there was *you*, with a silver trumpet at your lips, playing under the red sky. When you played the highest note, suddenly the floor of the castle split open, and out came a beautiful young woman.

KARI   Like you

SISSA   I'm as old as I'll ever be.

KARI   So am I.

SISSA   (*She holds out the cornet. KARI takes it.*) Play for me!

             PETUR *enters.*

PETUR   Hi. Seen my camera? (*KARI ignores him.*) I tried to
             warn you.

SISSA   (*brings him the camera*) Here it is. Take a picture of Kari
             playing to me!

PETUR   No.

SISSA   Please?! (*poses sensuously beside KARI*)

PETUR   All right. (*opens camera*)

KARI   (*freezes tensely while he shoots*) Are you going to marry
             her?

SISSA   Well she hasn't said yes yet, but she will.

PETUR   Sissa!

KARI   (*smiles*) Oh. It's *not* a done deal?

PETUR   It will be! Sorry you had to find out like that. I'll be
             sleeping at Prila's from now on. She won't come here
             now that– (*picks up his notebook and speaks brightly*)
             Well, I'm off. Got an interview at the base. (*looks at
             KARI*) There's a whole new world out there! (*goes*)

SISSA   (*to KARI*) *You* don't think I'm a half-wit, do you?

KARI   You see more than anyone knows, don't you? You're
             just like me.

SISSA   Bad?

KARI   We hear the music.

SISSA   What do you mean?

KARI   The place you go when life gets too–

SISSA   Real?

KARI   Hard.

SISSA   Was it hard in Copenhagen?

KARI   We drank champagne with beautiful ladies with ruby red lipstick and drowned out the sound of the tanks and the marching of boots with hot jazz and blues.

SISSA   You weren't afraid of them?

KARI   We should have been. It was just a matter of time. Our horn player was the first.

SISSA   What happened?

KARI   I was coming to play at the club one night. And a German truck was pulling away full of prisoners. I heard his voice, but when I turned around the truck had gone. His cornet was on his chair, as if he'd just laid it down. There was a note. "Kari, learn to play like Bix Beiderbecke, and this cornet is yours."

SISSA   Who is Beiderbecke?

KARI   The greatest player of them all. Now he plays with the angels. Listen to the master. (*puts on Beiderbecke tune quietly*) Give me that ribbon. (*She takes the ribbon from her hair, and he uses it to polish the cornet.*) This is the altar cloth. I rub it over her to warm her up. Look how I clean the valves. (*takes a valve out*) First, I make a mouthful of spit–

SISSA   Like this? (*shows him her tongue*)

KARI   (*He holds the valve out to her to drop the spit on.*) Let it drip onto the valve. Now I move it around, and screw it in, not too tight. See the pretty tops on the valves? That's Mother of Pearl, from a little creature far away in the South Seas.

SISSA   (*touches them*) Mother of Pearl!

KARI   Hold it against your lips. Press.

SISSA   (*She does.*) It's like kissing.

KARI   (*plays a few notes*) And when she is full of my wetness, I flip her over and press this– (*presses the drip lever*) See? Holy water.

SISSA   Give me a name.

KARI   Bring me your sister.

SISSA   I promise.

KARI   (*opens the drip lever, and lets water fall onto SISSA's forehead*) I name you – Billie Holiday.

SISSA   Billie Holiday! I am christened! I *knew* you were God!

> She runs into the street. *"Any Ol' Time"* sung by Billie Holiday. We hear Americani voices in the street. PRILA enters.

Prila! Kari wants you.

PRILA   Go home Sissa

SOLDIERS (*off*) Hello Gorgeous! Wanna smoke? Hey beautiful! (*whistles*) Man, look at those legs! Hey sister! You speaka American? (*whistles*)

SISSA   (*runs off towards the voices, trying to speak "American"*) Hi, Americani! I Billie Holiday! OK. Chewing gum, Wait for me seegarrett! [Cigarette]

> *PRILA enters KARI's parlour.*

KARI   (*turns and sees her, then turns back to play*) "Willow tree, hear my plea When you weep weep for me 'Cos I'm so weary with misery"

PRILA   He asked me to go to America.

Pause.

KARI   (*sings*) "On me it rains and rains
Each day brings aches and pains
Feel like a stranger everywhere
Nobody seems to care
The burden's more than I can bear"
(*He stops and turns.*) That was *our* dream.

PRILA   Petur will make it come true.

KARI   I was too late.

PRILA   Too late? You think this is all about timing? You think I waited for you until I lost hope, then settled for your brother? I gave you up the day you left. All those things you promised we'd do together – it was a big lie.

KARI   I'm not the same man who left. Please believe–

PRILA   –And of course Auntie Anna simply sent her little genius to Denmark. How convenient!

KARI   You're being cruel

PRILA   *I'm* being cruel??

KARI   I've stopped drinking.

PRILA   When? This morning?

KARI   When I left here.

PRILA   You've been sober for two years?

KARI   They were the longest years of my life. You're all I have left

PRILA   Your music means nothing?

KARI   Nothing without you. Have you really stopped singing?

PRILA   What are you running away from in Denmark?

KARI   I'm just coming home. To you.

PRILA   (*sarcastically*) Two years with no word, then suddenly
           I jump back into your mind?

KARI   You never left it! (*He moves towards her.*)

PRILA   It's over.

KARI   It never will be. Let's leave this place together, and
           sail to New York. Find our kind of people. The
           creatures of rhythm and melody. We'll make love
           to the music of Billie and Hoagy.

PRILA   Not any more.

KARI   Did you tell my brother you were coming here?

PRILA   No.

KARI   Good. (*He goes to the piano, plays and sings softly, "Sea
           Blue Sea."*)

PRILA   Don't!

KARI   Our song. Nobody else's. (*sings*)
           "Sea Blue Blue sea, Ocean of a dreamer's eye"
           (*to PRILA*) Sing.

           *PRILA pauses at the door, then leaves quickly. She
           stands outside listening and looking out to sea.*

Raven Canyon Radio Station. Same time of day.

           PETUR enters and listens.

JIM   (*on radio microphone*) Just last night, Squadron
           Leader Bill H. Anderson took the lead with the first
           American air strike of the Atlantic. His Squadron 269
           Hudson dropped its 250-pound depth charge right
           on top of a U-boat tailing a troop ship. When the sub
           started to sink, the first men to leave the boat were

not crew, but German officers. Well that says it
all, doesn't it? You won't find our commanders
abandoning their men. Our mother brought us up to
face the music. More news shortly. This is Jim Swing
signing off. (*JIM looks up and sees PETUR.*)

PETUR   (*in Icelandic accent*) Good day, Petur Karlsson, *Morning News*.

JIM   Howdy.

PETUR   This is the first I hear of the war. They have forbidden any news reports in the town.

JIM   But we set up a Big Band program for your radios at night.

PETUR   Yes! We heard a new melody last night. Good for dancing.

JIM   You speak our language great – for a foreigner. Did you learn it at school?

PETUR   Most of us learn by going to the bio (*pronounced bee-oh*)

JIM   Bee-oh?

PETUR   Film theatre. But I specialized in English in school.
I have a scholarship to study American literature in
Boston. *Harrvarrd.*

JIM   You must be pretty damned smart. (*whips a comb out of his pocket, straightens his uniform*) OK, shoot!

PETUR   Thank you. (*JIM poses. PETUR lines up and shoots.*)
I look very much forward to having some discussions
with Americans about books and poetry. I have
translated Hemingway, T.S. Eliot, Eugene O'Neill. You
would perhaps know the work of John Steinbeck? He
shaped my political thinking.

JIM   Ah, not so fast, buddy! What are you talking about?

PETUR   His view of the underbelly of capitalism.

JIM   Uh – I'm more of a movie man, myself. Want a serious picture? (*He tries to look brooding.*)

PETUR   Smiles are better. We want to show you are happy to be here. (*whips out a notebook*) Tell me your first impression of our country.

JIM   Well, no offence, but – I feel like I'm at the end of a long dirt road on the edge of a cliff.

PETUR   You are. But we have a magnificent landscape. Over to the east, there is a yellow sulphur mountain, with boiling blue mud under it. The smell is a little strong, like bad eggs, but it is remarkable.

JIM   Maybe I'll just try some fishing.

PETUR   Fishing is good, under the night-time sun. Nobody sleeps at night.

JIM   Bonanza!

PETUR   Bo-nanza–?

JIM   Know any girls you can introduce me to? I kinda want to get the jump on the other guys–

          Pause.

PETUR   I see you are unfamiliar with our ways, so I will explain our customs.

JIM   That'll be a help.

PETUR   Our women are independent and do not like to be told what to do. You cannot just – help yourself, as if it is a shoe shop. In your country a woman needs a man for happiness.

JIM   Of course.

PETUR   But in our culture, women value pride over happiness.

JIM And what about you. Are you guys like that?

PETUR Yes. Well we are very happy, of course, to see you have brought good weather and many jobs to our little town of Strandvik. And we look forward with large pleasure to attending your uh – Big Band Bash on Saturday night. This is the night of Midsummer. Strandvik has always celebrated the midnight sun with the biggest dance of the year. But we have decided to cancel our own dance, and accept your invitation.

JIM Buddy! You got it wrong! We ain't inviting the men. We're just going to borrow your gals for the night.

PETUR Borrow? What is this?

JIM It's good for morale. Cheer up the homesick soldiers. You *sure* don't want to see two thousand US soldiers making the move on your local women at your *own* dance!

PETUR There must be some mistake.

JIM We ain't asking the *married* ones. That would be disrespectful. You married?

PETUR You do not seem to understand some things. Iceland has a political arrangement with the United States.

JIM Huh?

PETUR We provide a re-fuelling stop for your aircraft and and destroyers, and–

JIM We protect you from Hitler – yeah but–

PETUR This arrangement also includes no involvement in the daily lives of the people.

JIM Unless they want it, and they will! Kari the jazz guy's gonna be a big draw.

PETUR Kari Jazzplayer?

JIM   He's gonna play at our Bash. We cooked it all up on the boat. An Icelandic Jazzman! That's pretty unreal–

PETUR   (*jumps in*) Oh no! He will play at our Midsummer Dance. It will not be cancelled now.

JIM   What are you? The Mayor?

PETUR   I am responsible for the plans.

JIM   Well – me too.

PETUR   You are guests.

JIM   Friends!

PETUR   Friends do not try to divide people. I suggest you cancel *your* Big Band Bash.

JIM   Look, pal–

PETUR   Petur.

JIM   Yeah, buddy. This was my idea. Don't get sore. You see I have this – philosophy. To keep folks happy, make 'em dance! (*beat*) Look, I'll get the fellas on the base to send a whole truckload of Southern Comfort to your little dance hall. You'll still have your uh – fiancees and wives at your dance. There's gotta be spare girls in this town. Share the wealth! We're not trying to make enemies with you guys. OK?

PETUR   Do not leave us to clean up your mess. (*He turns to go.*)

JIM   We don't leave a mess! We're Americans!

PETUR   You have one other thing very wrong. It is not I who am the foreigner. It is *you*. (*He leaves.*)

        PRILA sings standing on the hill overlooking the harbour while KARI is in the parlour playing piano.

PRILA &
KARI "Sea, blue blue sea, Ocean of a dreamer's eye
Show me what's beyond the place where your arms
touch the sky
I see a straight and broad highway, holding out its
hand
Burn little boat burn the way, burn to my dreamland

Sea blue blue sea rock me in your lover's bliss
Take away that old old pain
with cold and icy kiss
Take me on that broad highway and to that other land
There I'll live and there I'll die
cradled in your hand

Turn away from land, turn away from shore
Turn into the midnight sun, and enter heaven's door
Sea blue blue sea, Sea blue blue sea–"

Afternoon Thursday. Petur and Kari's Parlour

PETUR goes into the parlour. KARI stops playing.

PETUR So you've promised to play for the Americanis at their "Big Band Bash." Did you know that they've only invited the women?

KARI And me.

PETUR Word's got out that you're home. People expect you to play at the Midsummer dance.

KARI Too bad. (*He starts to polish his cornet.*)

PETUR I was planning to write an article for tomorrow's paper that you're making a big comeback at *our* dance.

KARI Then you'll look like an idiot if I don't show up.

PETUR You can't do this!

KARI This is my chance. To learn about Americani music. Make contacts.

PETUR   You feel no responsibility–?

KARI   (*cuts him off*) And maybe Prila will join me. A – reunion.

> *PETUR snaps and snatches the cornet out of KARI's hands and holds it as if he's going to throw it. KARI tenses up. An electric pause.*

I wouldn't do that. It would be as bad as stealing my woman.

> *PETUR lowers the cornet. KARI takes it from him.*

Don't touch it again. Ever.

PETUR   And don't touch *her* again – ever. (*He leaves.*)

Later Thursday afternoon.

> *PRILA in kitchen at the exchange.*

PRILA   Yes Svana! Did you read the invitation? Petur is cancelling the Midsummer Dance! Yes. Can you *imagine* dancing to an Americani *band*! Everyone'll go – *don't* go with Ingi! He's not your husband yet! Can you imagine dancing with some men who *don't* fall down before the night is over. What are you – no one wants to go bare-legged? How do you plan to do that? *Well*! I wouldn't be seen *dead* taking stockings from the Americanis!

SISSA   (*bursts in*) Prila! I found a soldier in the yard! Look! Cigarettes, chocolate, silk stockings! (*pours an armful of silk stockings, cigarettes and chocolate on the floor*) This is my sister, Prila!

PRILA   Get him out of here! Mamma's just out in the cow shed. She could come back in any minute!

SISSA   He's lonely! Come in, Soldier!

JIM   (*enters*) Pardon me for troublin' ya. I'll go if you want, but I just gotta say – I sure hope you ain't mad at me for starin' at ya – I just can't help myself – you are *beeeautifull*!

SISSA   What's he saying?

PRILA   Get him out!

SISSA   I'll keep Mamma busy. I know! I'll offer to help her, that'll slow her down.

> *SISSA gallops off. JIM stands in the entrance.*

JIM   You speak American?

PRILA   Yes. Goodbye

JIM   That's great! I couldn't understand a word *she* was saying.

PRILA   These (*indicates stockings and stuff*) are yours?

JIM   A beautiful gal like you should wear silk.

> *PRILA picks the stuff out and throws it out into the yard.*

Man – you're a tough cookie!

PRILA   I do not need a friend.

JIM   Kari sent me.

PRILA   (*startled*) Kari?

JIM   He hitched a ride up the coast on our boat. He said you might sing with our band on Saturday. See we don't got no dames in the army. A gal singer would be BONANZA!

PRILA   Bonanza?

JIM   *I'm* the drummer. (*beat*) I played in bands back home in Kansas.

PRILA   Do you know Hoagy Carmichael?

JIM   Uh – sure! I've played with the greats. Started on
          crew, and made my way up. (*He starts drumming
          with cutlery he finds on the table. It is quite flashy and
          impresses PRILA.*) One day, I'll take you to hear the
          Kansas City Six. When I get home I'm gonna follow
          in the footsteps of Jo Jones, Big Sid Catlett, Gene
          Krupa! *Old friends!*

PRILA   (*laughs*) You do not need drums!

JIM   Hands, and feet, while my heart keeps the beat! Pa!
          pa pabada da daddowapada! (*drumming on everything
          in sight*) When I was a kid I drummed the table, the
          chair, the floor, the legs. (*drums on his legs*) The GIRLS!
          (*He does a flourish on her back. PRILA enjoys it.*) So. I'm
          – ah – looking to be shown around by a beautiful girl
          like you. Any chance?

PRILA   You are trying to buy me.

JIM   I'm sorry you feel that way. My mamma always told
          me, "Never overstay your welcome." (*He kisses her
          hand and leaves. On the way down the hill he meets
          PETUR on his way to PRILA's.*) Hi, buddy!

PETUR   My name is Petur.

JIM   Uh – yeah, I know. Are you – still mad?

PETUR   I am perfectly sane.

JIM   Look, we got off to a bad start. I want to be friends.
          I guess you and your friends still have your noses
          out of joint about the dance.

PETUR   Noses?

JIM   I might have had second thoughts, you know, invited
          the couples and all, but after talking to you, I don't
          think US soldiers and Icelandic guys are a good mix at
          a dance – do you?

PETUR   Now you are piling injury on top of the insult! (*laughs*) I would *never* go back to the Strandvik men and tell them– "Oh the Americani has had a second thought and we are permitted to come!" Icelandic men too, have their pride.

JIM   Glad we agree on something. I'm not out to insult anybody. Shake? (*PETUR doesn't.*) I'm startin' to catch on to this pride thing. That angel in the big house on the cliff – she's got a bad case.

PETUR   Prila?

JIM   I'm trying to get her to sing at the Big Band Bash.

PETUR   Do not go to that house again.

JIM   She your–? (*disappointed*) Aw shucks! Might have guessed she'd be *somebody's* gal. Hey! You could *sweet-talk* her into singin' at our dance!

PETUR   Sweet-talk is for hypocrites. (*He leaves.*)

JIM   It works in the USA! (*He goes off whistling.*)

Prila's house. Thursday early evening.

PETUR   (*coming in*) What's going on?

PRILA   Northern Iceland telephone. Kristín! Are you going to the Americani Bash?

PETUR   Prila?

PRILA   Dzindzer Rodzers? Great! Those soldiers have got style, you know. The girls are excited about it.

PETUR   You're not going to sing at this Big Band Bash with Kari, are you?

PRILA   (*to PETUR*) What?

PETUR   That stupid Jim Swing Prick thinks I'm going to
         encourage that! Doesn't even know his own literature,
         and he thinks he can organize a dance for two
         thousand soldiers?! He's got a nerve, coming in here
         and trying to seduce you, of *all* people. Well. He met
         his match, didn't he?

PRILA   Why are you so upset?

PETUR   Oh I'm not! They're trying to get all the local girls out
         to their "Bash" – but they're not inviting us men! It
         won't work of course. You just have to let your
         friends all know the Big Band Bash is off limits.
         I'll talk to the Strandvik men.

PRILA   Petur! The local guys would *hate* to be at the same
         dance as those soldiers, watching them put the make
         on the girls. (*laughs*) The competition would drive the
         Strandvik boys crazy. Especially since half of them are
         working for the Americanis.

PETUR   Prila! You're not thinking straight.

         HILDUR enters.

PRILA   (*angry*) Just because you've changed your mind, all
         the girls have to suddenly go along with you? When
         did you start to think we'd take orders?

HILDUR   She's prickly isn't she? You'll have to go along with
         her ways if you marry her. She's not used to having a
         man around. This is a women's household.

PETUR   I'm aware of that, Hildur.

HILDUR   You come from good stock. I keep your father's
         poetry book beside my bed! She's a lucky girl.

PRILA   *I'll* decide if I'm lucky! (*turns to PETUR*) *and* I'll
         decide whether I sing!

HILDUR   (*puts on her gum boots and gets a bucket and a mop*) I
         hear your brother's back. I'm surprised he didn't
         drown himself in liquor yet.

PRILA   Keep your nose out of it!

HILDUR   (*to PETUR*) See? *Prickly!*

PRILA   (*to PETUR*) You can't solve every problem in the world! Now go tell the Strandvik boys to take it easy. (*kisses him, ushers him out and rushes back to telephone*) Oh! I'm sorry! Putting you through – Hallo? Hallo?

> *KARI is playing instrumental lead-in to "Stardust" on piano.*

Thursday Night.

Sounds of Hiddenfolk.

SISSA   (*speaking to the Hiddenfolk girl*) I have lots of lovely presents for you, when you come out. You'll be wearing silky stockings, and perfume, and look! Cigarettes! All for us! We'll save them for the Americani Bash! We'll go together with our Hollywood soldiers! I'll have Clark Gable, and you can have Jimmy Stewart! I'm going to be Bette Davis. I borrowed the dress from Prila. Don't tell! Oh my heart feels so big and loud, I think if I don't make mad passionate love with a beautiful soldier soon, I'm going to *burst!* (*ladles out wine from the barrel to invisible people*) Anyone want a drink? It makes you happy. (*slurps a huge ladle of red currant wine*) Now, everybody! It's time for the battle plan! We must think of a way to get Mamma to let me have a confirmation ceremony. Think! Drink! (*listens to whispering*) Yes? Yes? Oh...

> *PRILA in her house sewing her dress and hearing the music. KARI sings as if he knows she can hear him.*

KARI   "Sometimes I wonder why I spend the lonely nights
Dreaming of a dream
The memory haunts my reverie
And I am once again with you
When our love was new, and each kiss an inspiration
Ah but that was long ago and now my consolation
Is in the stardust of a song...."

*"Stardust" continues, and runs softly under the next
scene instrumentally. PRILA is drawn across town
towards KARI during the following speech. It is as if
the words HILDUR is saying are running through
PRILA's mind.*

*HILDUR is holding a man's jacket, and lays it down
on the bed. It is ten o'clock. The sky is crimson with
the night sun.*

HILDUR   Ohh Haraldur, my darling you came home. Your little
girl was waiting for you. (*smells the jacket*) Oh so
good.

*Sighs. SISSA hears her mother's voice. The band
continues to play a soft instrumental in the
background.*

Oh my darling let me just look at you. My man my
man, my man. Come back home my darling. Lie
beside me and stroke my hair. I'm so empty without
you. Wake me up. Fill the emptiness between my
thighs.... Oh my sweet man. Why could I not save
you? Why did you leave me all alone when you said
you loved me so? Why? Take me with you when you
leave, take me, take me, take me with you – Ooohh.
Oh God– (*sees SISSA standing in front of her*) Aaagh!
How long have you been here?!

SISSA   You sounded like you were dying.

HILDUR   You're having one of your dreams.

SISSA   Maybe I am, but I'm still awake. Call me Billie.

HILDUR   You're mad.

SISSA   The Hiddenfolk are back, Mamma. And they're
angry! They won't leave unless I get confirmed.

HILDUR   You little *schemer*!

SISSA   And if you won't let me get confirmed, I'll tell
everybody that you cry for Father and make love
with yourself. (*starts to leave*)

HILDUR   *No*! Go ahead. Have your Confirmation!

SISSA   Thank you Mother.

PETUR   (*coming into the house, SISSA waltzes up to him*) Sissa where's your sister?

SISSA   Petur! I'm going to have a confirmation! You're invited.

PETUR   (*calling*) Prila!

HILDUR   (*comes in*) Is there no sleeping in this house?

PETUR   I have to talk to Prila. Do you know where she is?

HILDUR   I thought she was with you. What's wrong with you?

PETUR   The Strandvik men have just heard they're not invited to the Americani Big Band Bash. They're furious! I need Prila's help to stop the girls from going–

HILDUR   In my day the way they controlled the women was to shame them! (*She leaves.*)

SISSA   I know where Prila is.

PETUR   Where?

> *Sissa runs off. PETUR follows.*

Petur and Kari's house.

> *KARI and JIM playing music.*

PRILA   (*singing*) "All of me
Why not take all of me
Can't you see,
I'm no good without you,
Take my lips, I want to lose them,
Take my arms, I'll never use them,
Your goodbye left me with eyes that cry,

How can I go on, dear, without you,
You took the part
That once was my heart,
So why not take all of me."

PETUR   (*calls off*) Prila!

> *He rushes in. The musicians stop playing. KARI stops*
> *playing, turns to him and smiles.*

ACT TWO

Thursday Night. 3AM.

PETUR, at the harbour. He is smoking, and very distraught. PRILA finds him.

PRILA   Why did you leave?

PETUR   Why should I stay? (*She doesn't answer.*) *Why* should I stay?

PRILA   To hear me sing?

PETUR   To hear you sing? To hear you sing—like that—with – the man who– I don't understand why you–

PRILA   I – missed it.

PETUR   Missed – it?

PRILA   When he played -- it was as if I woke up.

PETUR   Oh. You've been asleep?

PRILA   No! Stop trying to make this wrong!

PETUR   Well, it sounds pretty strange to be told by the woman whom you plan to marry–

PRILA   Plan?

PETUR   –That she was sleeping for the last year.

PRILA   I was not asleep! But a *part* of me was!

PETUR   Don't tell me which part!

PRILA   How dare you!

PETUR   How dare I?

PRILA   How can you stand there and talk to me like that! It's not you.

PETUR   But this is the new you?

PRILA   This is just me! Who I always was.

PETUR   I'm having trouble believing what I'm hearing. The man who nearly killed you in a drunken fit, then left—for two years—now conveniently comes back to *wake you up* and pick up where he left off–

PRILA   Stop! You promised *never* to bring up the past!

PETUR   What about *you*?

PRILA   Don't do this! (*Pause.*) Petur – I can't stand to see you so mean – and cold. Tell me how you feel.

PETUR   Can't you see?

> *KARI arrives. He stands behind PETUR, who does not see him.*

Are you trying to make a fool of me?

KARI   Prila, are you coming? (*PETUR turns and he and KARI stare at each other.*)

PRILA   Petur, what do *you* want? (*steps towards him, he does not move*) You have to tell me how you feel right now!

PETUR   You – picked the wrong time to ask.

PRILA   (*turns to KARI*) Alright. Let's go! (*She turns, cold and hard. Beat. The men stare at each other.*) Come on!! (*KARI follows her. They join JIM and get ready for a practice.*)

> *PETUR takes another cigarette. SISSA comes charging towards him.*

SISSA   Oooh! Americani cigarettes! Can I have one? (*He crushes the pack and steps on it.*) Oh now look what you did! (*She scrambles for the pack and pulls one out.*) It's broken! (*with a bent cigarette in her mouth*) Gotta light, soldier?

PETUR   Get *up* Sissa! Have some self-respect! (*He picks her up roughly.*)

SISSA   What's that?

PETUR   (*starts to go*) Never mind.

SISSA   I heard the men talking at the statue of Mattias the poet. They said "Petur's going to stop the Americani Bash. He's smart. He knows what to do." (*PETUR turns back to her.*) Tell me.

PETUR   They want me to publish the names of the girls who go to the Americani Bash. In the *Morning News*.

SISSA   *Will* you?

PETUR   We'll see. (*He starts to go.*)

SISSA   I want to go to the Americani Bash! I want to be in the newspaper! (*runs to him and drapes herself on him*) And take a picture of me with my Hollywood soldier!

PETUR   You don't understand!

SISSA   I do! I see everything! Ask me! (*He pushes her away and leaves.*)

Sissa in the Cellar.

In the cellar, SISSA speaks to the girl under the floor.

SISSA   Oh, my friend, I'm not sure if it's safe for you to come out any more! Everything is going so strange and I don't know what's real. You Hiddenfolk only appear when you have to show your feelings. That makes you real. I heard you crying all my life and so I *know* you're real. That's what makes me real too, doesn't it? But everybody's lying about how they feel. I know, because I *feel inside* them. Petur is supposed to feel love, like Jimmy Stewart, but I felt something more and it made me want to die. Why does it hurt so much? Oh! Oh! Help me! Prila! Run away! Oh you have to escape! But you don't want to! (*weeps*) Something's breaking. Why is it all so sad? Love should make us happy. Don't they know that? You know my friend, I think our Hollywood soldiers are the only people who understand that. (*wipes her eyes*) They'll make everything alright. They'll keep us safe.

Wind whistles and the sky changes colour.

Band Plays a Warm-up Improv.

JIM   Guys! I've got this great new song, hot from the USA. Here's the chart. It starts like this. Everyone sing – Woo woo! Kari. You sing do you?

KARI   (*sings*) Woo woo.

JIM   Great! We'll start in three-part with the woos, then–

PRILA   Jim, vot is this that makes the woo woo.

JIM   Oh. The Choo choo.

PRILA   Tsoo tsoo?

JIM   Yeah. Choo choo.

PRILA   Explain–

JIM   Uhh – oh, you guys don't have trains here, do you? Man! That's so – you've never seen one for real! (*PRILA and KARI wait as he searches for an explanation.*) Well, it's a kind of a long bus that travels on steel rods... with other buses attached to it. It's real big— and loud—full of people and goes Woo! Woo!

KARI   This is a locomotive.

JIM   (*startled*) Oh *yeah*! OK! Can we start?

KARI   Ready.

JIM   Now, me and Lance'll start up the rhythm, then Kari, kick in with the keyboard, OK? OK. 1-2-3 cook!

They start the intro. Singing whoo whoo in harmony.

PRILA   (*sings*) Parrdon mee boyss, is that the tsatanooga tsoo tsoo? (*stops singing*) Jim, Tsatanooga, vot is this?

JIM   Oh, it's a place in America.

KARI   Tsattanooga Tennessee.

JIM   (*impressed*) Yes!

PRILA   A town like this?

JIM   Not exactly. It's in the USA. I'll take you there sometime, sweetheart.

KARI   Are we ready?

JIM   Oh yes! One-two-three fry!

They start again.

PRILA   (*sings*) Pardon mee boyss, is that the tsatanooga tsoo tsooo.

JIM   (*sings*) Yes, yes, track twenty-nine.

PRILA   (*sings*) Boy vood you giff me a shine? (*stops singing*) Jim?

JIM   (*stops playing*) Yes?

PRILA   Vott is a shine?

JIM   Oh. Ah – when someone shines your shoes for you.

PRILA   People in America have dirty shoes?

JIM   No, they ah, they just do that in stations.

PRILA	Who?
JIM	Shoe-shine boys. It's a job.
PRILA	And you pay them?
JIM	Yes.
PRILA	You cannot do it yourself?
JIM	You see, in America, people don't have the time. They've gotta catch the *train – see*? (*beat*) OK! 1-2-3 sizzle!
PRILA	(*sings*) There's gonna be a certain parrtee at the station Satin and lace I used to call fonnee face– (*stops singing*) Jim! A parrtee at the station?
JIM	Yeah, like a bus station.
PRILA	You heff parrtees in stations?
JIM	A party in this case, is a person.
PRILA	And you call a parrtee fonny face?
JIM	You call a person a party.
PRILA	A person vith a fonnee face is a parrtee?
JIM	It's a way of saying she's you know – cute! Like you.
KARI	Is this a practice?
PRILA	*My* face is fonnee?
JIM	*No!* I–
KARI	You have a song to learn, fonnee-face.
PRILA	I haff to understand vott I sing.

JIM   (*yelling*) It makes sense when you sing it, *honest!*
               1-2-3–

PRILA   So. I am singing a song, about going in a long bus,
               vith shiny shoes, to meet a fonnee face, but who is
               not a partee and not having a partee, but is called a
               partee?

JIM   But she's this great gal, you see, she's the *reason* for
               the *song*... this guy is rushing for the train, getting all
               dandied up, dreaming about the little lady waiting
               for him in Chattanooga... (*desperately*) You guys gotta
               believe me it's a *big hit* in the States! It'll catch on
               here! It will *I promise you!*

               JIM starts the drum rhythm again.

PRILA   Jim. (*He stops.*) Does it maybe sound something like
               this?

JIM   What?

               PRILA and KARI sing the "woo"s.

PRILA   (*sings with a good attempt at an American accent*)
               "Pardon me boys is that the Chattanooga Choo choo?

KARI   (*sings*) Yes, yes, track twenty-nine,

PRILA   Boy would you give me a shine.
               There's gonna be a certain party at the station,
               Satin and lace,

KARI   I used to call funny-face–

               *PRILA and KARI collapse laughing. JIM sees the
               practise is over, picks up his drum, knowing the joke
               was on him, but taking it well.*

JIM   I just don't get you guys!

               Music segues to something soft on the radio.

6AM **Friday.**

JIM   (*at Raven Canyon Radio*) Another non-stop day on the edge of the world! Have you guys noticed that no one seems to go to bed around here? Birds singing all night, little kids playing in the street at 3AM – kinda like a dream, isn't it? Like the juices never stop flowing. Well, let's keep 'em flowing till Saturday night. I've got a special guest in the studio today. You guys in barracks 66 remember the crazy Icelander blowing his horn on the bow of the ship in that wild Atlantic storm? Buddy, you were either fearless, or drunk! Well, he's playing the dance tomorrow, and I hear, where Kari plays, the girls come – flocking! (*Kari laughs.*) Kari Jazz. Cool Cat, say howdy to the fellas.

KARI   Hallo my friends from the boat! We will have a good time again tomorrow night.

JIM   Kari, let me ask you on behalf of the guys on the base, how do you say "I love you" to a woman in your language?

KARI   This is not usually spoken by men in Iceland. We do not demonstrate romance.

JIM   Well, that's a handy little tip, thanks. So what's the magic key, Kari, to giving the Icelandic girls the night of their life?

KARI   Good American music. A woman will do everything for a man who puts jazz in her blood.

JIM   And that's what it's all about! Here's a taste of things to come. Kari Jazzplayer, Pied Piper of Iceland, tickling the ivories for you–

        KARI starts to play "Any Ol' Time", and the sound transfers to the radio in HILDUR's kitchen.

8AM **Friday.**

HILDUR's kitchen.

PETUR enters. HILDUR comes in from the henhouse carrying a basket.

HILDUR Prila's not here professor. She went to town to get a cod.

PETUR I'll wait.

PRILA comes in furious and slaps a cod wrapped in brown paper on the table.

PRILA (*to PETUR*) Why didn't you tell me?!

HILDUR Did Skipper Lalli like the eggs?

PRILA He wants cash for his fish next time.

HILDUR I don't have any cash.

PRILA Then get a job!! (*to PETUR*) The whole town's talking and I'm the last to know.

HILDUR Know what?

PRILA Your professor is planning on humiliating every girl in Strandvik, Mamma.

HILDUR (*to PETUR*) How?

PRILA By publishing the name of any of the women who go to the Big Band Bash instead of the Midsummer dance.

HILDUR In the *newspaper*?

PRILA What the hell do you think you're doing, Petur?

PETUR I *tried* to tell you. If you weren't so busy with your – music.

PRILA   So let me get this straight. You and the men of Strandvik have decided that because the Americanis have invited women only to their Big Band Bash, they're stealing your property?

PETUR   This is not a simple issue, Prila. The honour of Strandvik is at stake. Can't you see what is happening? All over town girls are being courted with smiles and gifts by men who talk like film stars! There are a lot of vulnerable girls who'll let these soldiers sweep them off their feet.

PRILA   Maybe it's because they know how to be romantic.

PETUR   That's not romance! It's just – sweet talk!

HILDUR   Oooh!

PETUR   They could have wives in America! Girls could end up with soldier babies who never know their fathers.

HILDUR   But how do you think humiliating the women will stop that?

PETUR   It's a *warning*! If the girls find out that their names will be in the paper for going to the Big Band Bash, then they'll change their minds and they won't go.

PRILA   Don't make predictions about us too soon.

PETUR   When the war is over and the Americans are gone, you'll see. All that'll be left is disappointment and heartbreak. You'll end up having to live with the local men who never could compete with that glamour. We'll never recover.

PRILA   You mean *you'll* never recover.

PETUR   No! I mean Strandvik! I won't let these foreigners destroy my home town, just because they think we're ignorant peasants!

HILDUR   Then tell *them*! They brought work and money. That's why you don't dare to confront them.

PRILA   You've picked on us, thinking that we'll be terrified to be publicly shamed! Well we won't. We're too busy cleaning up after the children and men to care about humiliation! We're the ones who scrape off the stink of fish and sour milk and dress ourselves up like film stars for the Saturday dances. Hiding our bare legs and red knees under our dresses.

HILDUR   Rita Haystack on the outside, poor as dirt underneath.

PRILA   Then spend the night *pretending* to ourselves that those drunken Strandvik boors are maybe going to show some glimmer of romance instead of drinking themselves into a coma!

PETUR   Not me!

PRILA   They tell us we're beautiful. That's new for us.

PETUR   They're buying Iceland and you girls have put yourselves up for sale!

PRILA   And you men have been getting it for free!

         Pause.

HILDUR   Maybe you're right. These soldiers are changing the rules in this town, and some girls will get sucked in. But you're just as bad, Petur. You are a leader in Strandvik, and you could have calmed things down. Instead you're inflaming them. Go back and tell the men there's nothing to do but wait.

PETUR   And risk this town drinking itself into a fury?

HILDUR   They do that *every* Saturday night!

PETUR   The way to control women was to shame them. Those were your words last night Hildur.

HILDUR   That was a statement of *fact*. Not a piece of advice, boy!

PRILA   You could just tie stones around our necks and throw us in the river like the old days! It's a lot simpler.

PETUR   Prila! You should take this seriously! The Strandvik girls will do what you do.

PRILA   Don't throw the responsibility on me!

PETUR   And don't throw it all on me! (*Beat. PETUR hands her the flier.*) This is what the men want.

PRILA   (*reads it*) "Warning to the women of Strandvik. All those who attend the Big Band Bash held by the Americani military will have their names published in the *Morning News* as Whores of the Americanis." (*looks up at him*) Whores? I never thought *you* would– Why are you doing this?

PETUR   *Someone* has to. (*to PRILA*) *Are* you going to sing at the Big Band Bash?

           PRILA tears up the flier and leaves. PETUR goes.

HILDUR   Well the war's finally come to our doorstep.

Raven Canyon.

           PRILA joins the band. During this SISSA comes down from the mountain with flowering thyme and starts getting ready for the party. HILDUR is in the kitchen.

PRILA   (*sings*) "Mamma said no
           Pappa said go
           But I never thought that you'd ever blow
           This town Bad boy
           When I was down Bad boy
           If you want to stay
           you'd better learn to play
           In Harmony.
           You're looking half dead
           You're ready for bed
           But I ain't tucking you in sleepy head, not yet

Bad Boy
I'm hard to get, bad boy
If you're gonna stay you'd better learn to play
In two-part harmony
So spread your fingers play those keys
Sing me some sweet songs down on your knees
You're gonna play play play
Every dog must have his day."

Friday Evening.

PRILA and JIM at the north end of the Fiord looking at the night sun.

JIM   Will the horses be OK there? They won't take off?

PRILA   I told them to wait for us.

JIM   And they agreed?

PRILA   Yes (*JIM is incredulous. She looks at him.*) They will. Did you like the ride?

JIM   I'll never forget it. Pretty frightening. They're like goats the way they climbed this cliff.

PRILA   You did well.

JIM   Thanks. I guess I've got your little sister to thank for introducing us. Man, she's a strange one. What makes her tick?

PRILA   She can speak to our other population. The ones who live in the mountains.

JIM   Huh?

PRILA   The Hiddenfolk.

JIM   She can see them?

PRILA   Most people cannot see them. We just know they are there. But my little sister has the gift.

JIM   You're spooking me.

PRILA   You do not need to be afraid, if you leave them alone.

JIM   Uh – thanks for the tip.

         *Realizes he's close to the cliff edge. PRILA is right on
         the edge. He yells.*

         Whoa! Gee! This is a sheer drop! Don't go so close!

PRILA   I am used to it.

JIM   So, straight ahead is the North Pole?

PRILA   The Arctic Circle.

JIM   That sun is like a big ball of fire. Does it sit there all
         night?

PRILA   Oh no. It will move over the ocean and go around to
         the east, then the sky will become like fire.

JIM   I haven't slept a wink since I got here.

PRILA   Nobody does for all summer.

JIM   The guys in Raven Canyon are feeling kinda crazy.
         Like kids in a candy shop that never closes. You
         know?

PRILA   This is normal. It is our gift, for getting through the
         winter of dark. Do you like it?

JIM   The colour of the sun! What do you call it?

PRILA   Red.

JIM   The colour of your lips. You are the most beautiful
         girl I've ever seen in my life.

PRILA   Why do Americans say "the most," always "the
         most" and always "the best"?

JIM   We're from the best country in the world, and we have the most bread, I guess.

PRILA   Bread?

JIM   Money, honey.

PRILA   Where you are from, do you have a big house and much bread?

JIM   Kansas? Oh no. Two-room farmhouse for Mom and ten kids. Dad rode the rails looking for jobs. Can't tell where he is now.

PRILA   Rails? This is choo choo! (*JIM laughs.*) You had a difficult time in your rich America.

JIM   I joined up so I could send money home to Mom and the kids. But there ain't no basic training that gets you ready for the real thing.

PRILA   What thing?

JIM   Three weeks on the north Atlantic hearing bombers over your head and not knowing if they're ours, 'cos the fog's so thick you can't tell the sky from the sea. We didn't fire till they did. We lost a ship.

PRILA   Are you – afraid?

JIM   (*beat*) I got a pocketful of cash and the best suit I ever owned. I'm only afraid of you. (*PRILA laughs.*) What did you tell your guy Peter about me? I don't plan on getting killed on neutral territory.

PRILA   What is there to tell?

JIM   Where I come from, if a girl gallops into the sunset with a strange guy, her boyfriend comes after them with guns blazing.

PRILA   Where I come from, the girl rides the horse faster.

JIM   (*looks out at the sky*) Oh *wow*! Oh oh look! Look at that! Hundreds of geese!

PRILA   Swans.

JIM   Wild swans?

PRILA   Yes.

JIM   I always thought they just floated around on ponds.

PRILA   They are trumpeter swans.

JIM   Times like this, I wish I was a poet.

PRILA   Maybe you are.

Music. The cornet rises above a soft jazz tune. The sound of swans increases, and finally fades away.

JIM   Oh, man, the sun's made their chests all red, like angels with bleeding hearts. I'm seeing heaven. I have fallen hopelessly in love with you.

PRILA   Now?

JIM   And for ever! I love you. (*He starts to dance with her, jiving, and drumming on her with his hands. He sings.*) "Oh say can you see, by the dawn's early light what so proudly we hailed at the twilight's last gleaming."

He pauses close enough to kiss her, then draws on all his inner strength to tear himself away. He leaves regretfully, saluting her, and humming. PRILA is left in the afterglow.

Friday evening. Hildur's kitchen.

Birds singing outside. The clock is ticking. HILDUR comes in from cooking area wiping her hands.

SISSA   Look! I picked violets and flowering thyme on the lava rocks, *and* I saw a Mamma ptarmigan with 14 babies! It's a sign.

HILDUR   Of what?

SISSA   From the Hiddenfolk, that it's going to be a wonderful 14th birthday.

HILDUR   It's just a sign of summer. This is ridiculous!

SISSA   Have you made all the waffles? We need rhubarb jam.

HILDUR   Yes, yes. (*goes off to kitchen area to get jam and waffles*)

SISSA   (*calls after her*) And after you've done that, you can leave.

HILDUR   How do you know people are coming?

SISSA   I wrote invitations and delivered them. I'm not stupid, Mamma.

HILDUR   You've found Prila's old confirmation dress. Looks pretty. She sneaked off to the church in that. Never told me.

SISSA   Hurry up. They won't come in if you're here. They're scared of you.

HILDUR   So they should be. There. That's all I'm serving. No smoked meat and rye bread. I don't have any time. This is such a rush.

SISSA   Mamma! You agreed to this. Now go!

HILDUR   I'll go up the mountain and look for mountain moss. I'll mix it in with the flat bread. (*she hesitates*) I'll be back in two hours.

SISSA   If they're still here, you can hide in the cellar.

HILDUR   I do *not* hide! (*leaves*)

Friday evening.

PRILA and KARI up the mountain.

KARI   You've saved me. You're my angel.

PRILA   Why now? Why couldn't I save you two years ago?

KARI   When I came to, that morning after the dance –
          I knew–

PRILA   –You remembered?

KARI   Yes.

PRILA   And you've never said anything.

KARI   Every time the memory came back I drank it away.

PRILA   How long have you been sober?

KARI   Long enough to know I'm never going back to it. I'm
          asking you to trust me.

PRILA   Kari! How would I begin–?

KARI   Listen. I have to tell you what I remember–

PRILA   Don't!

KARI   I found myself standing with a broken bottle in my
          hand. You were lying on the ground, your face
          covered in blood. I knew that morning it was all over.

PRILA   For you or me?

KARI   I – tried to kill myself. My aunt found me. It's taken
          me two years to get the courage to ask you–

PRILA   To forgive you?

KARI   Yes! When I'm with you I don't need anything else.

PRILA   You haven't told me the whole truth, have you? What are you coming back from?

       Beat.

KARI   I – lost a month. Everything was falling apart. I had to get out of Denmark. I was afraid I'd try it again. You're the only one who makes me feel like living.

PRILA   You're asking me to forgive you for the wrong thing. I know what drinking does to you. What you did to me that night of the dance – it could have been anybody you attacked. But if you'd stayed, I would never let it happen again. And it's true. I could have saved you from wanting to kill yourself. But you left me behind without a word. You're not the only one who wanted to die.

KARI   I'm sorry.

PRILA   You killed my hopes. Your brother brought them back.

KARI   (*moves close, ready to kiss her*) Prila, I'm here now. (*She feels the heat.*) He'll never know you like I do. Do you really want to follow his dream or ours?

       PRILA surrenders to the passion, and they lock into an intense embrace. The old fire awakened. HILDUR suddenly appears.

HILDUR   Prila!

PRILA   How long have you been here?

HILDUR   Long enough to see what a fool you are.

PRILA   Kari, leave. (*She stares at HILDUR. HILDUR leaves in the other direction.*)

Kari and Petur's Parlour.

PETUR is sitting at the piano. He has a bottle of liquor and two glasses.

KARI   (*enters*) Expecting company?

PETUR   Waiting for you.

KARI   I hear you're trying to sabotage the Americani dance.

PETUR   And you've manipulated Prila into singing for you?

KARI   *With* me. I haven't done anything you wouldn't expect me to do. You're the unpredictable one.

PETUR   I – bought a ticket to America.

KARI   Just one?

PETUR   It's your chance. Take it.

KARI   My chance for what?

PETUR   What you've always wanted.

KARI   No. Thanks.

PETUR   Aunt Anna will cut you off, and you'll never raise the cash. So choose. Stay here for the rest of your life playing Saturday dances with amateurs, or–

KARI   Leave her for you. Are you sure she–

PETUR   (*cuts him off*) Just think about it. Kari! Come on! Let's not be enemies. Have a drink.

KARI   No. That's over.

PETUR   (*laughs*) I know you better! Just a toast! To better days! (*pours two glasses*)

KARI   What are you trying to do?

PETUR   Make peace.

KARI   (*laughs*) Petur politician! You've got a plan for
            everything don't you? By the time you save the
            world, there won't be any music left in it.

PETUR   You're lecturing *me*?!

KARI   You saw how happy she was, singing again, didn't
            you? (*beat*) Little brother, you are confused.

PETUR   I trust her. And I believe in what I have to do. I love
            her in a way you never will, and we both know it.

KARI   Whom does she love? Are you afraid to ask?

PETUR   Choose.

> *PETUR puts the ticket on the piano and leaves.
> KARI picks up the ticket and reads it. He pauses
> momentarily in front of the glass of liquor, then downs
> it in one. As he does, the clock begins to chime ten. He
> puts the ticket in the cornet case. The sound of the
> clock gets louder.*

Friday Night. In the Kitchen.

> *SISSA, wearing PRILA's white confirmation dress,
> sits and waits. Time has passed, the clock chimes to
> ten. HILDUR enters and stands looking at SISSA.*

SISSA   Why do they hate me?

HILDUR   It's not you they hate.

SISSA   You knew they wouldn't come.

HILDUR   Yes.

SISSA   Tell me why! (*shouting*) Mamma tell me! (*Pause.*) I'll
            go and find out for myself! I'll ask every person in
            town "what did I do to make you hate me?"

HILDUR *No*! Don't. (*beat*) You want to know why no one comes near this house? You want to be grown up?

SISSA Yes.

HILDUR I was called marriage devil. Your brothers and Prila came home bloody with fighting. I couldn't tell them the truth till they were older. I couldn't bear my children to hate me.

SISSA They never told me.

HILDUR It was all before you were born. You were never to know.

SISSA Why not?

HILDUR You're – different. You – you make up stories. You would talk about it all the time, and I couldn't stand that.

SISSA What's a marriage devil?

HILDUR (*She summons the courage.*) Your father had another family when he met me. I was just a girl. I worked up in the fields drying the fish. He was old enough to be my father. He used to walk up and down the rows of girls, supervising us. They say I stole him. I didn't. I fell in love.

SISSA What was it like?

HILDUR Don't make me say–

SISSA You've never told me anything. I need to know. What did it feel like?

HILDUR It was like a fire that started to burn, and wouldn't go out. We – were drawn together, as if we had one soul.

SISSA Is that why you pretend to make love with him in the night? Why you cry?

HILDUR	He died when I was still young – so full of – oh you can't understand.
SISSA	When it started – did you try to stop? Really try?
HILDUR	No. I *knew* it was wrong. But the feeling he gave me. I couldn't fight it. Nothing – nobody else mattered
SISSA	What happened to his other family?
HILDUR	The children were sent to farms in the west fiords.
SISSA	And his wife?
HILDUR	Greta. They found her at the bottom of this cliff. Washed up by the tide. People said I was the one who should have died.
SISSA	So they act as if you did. You like it this way don't you?
HILDUR	Yes. But the dead don't let you forget them.
SISSA	And now everybody says you're wicked.
HILDUR	Yes.
SISSA	But it was his fault.
HILDUR	Don't you make anyone bad. We had six beautiful children.
SISSA	Six?
HILDUR	How could it have been bad?
SISSA	But now you have a rock in your heart for ever.
HILDUR	Better a rock in my heart than throwing myself off a cliff and leaving my children alone.
SISSA	But you put me outside in the field alone.
HILDUR	How do you know that?

SISSA   Prila found me. You put me out to die when I was
            born. *Why?*

HILDUR   I – woke up in the night. In his arms. He was holding
            me so tight, I couldn't breathe. He never made a
            sound. Just turned blue. Then I felt the pain. You
            came out *hungry*! Screaming for my milk. I had
            nothing to give. We lay together in a dead man's bed.
            You at my feet screaming for me. Me screaming for
            him. I – just – couldn't–

SISSA   Seven, Mamma, not six. You had seven beautiful
            children. Counting me.

> *SISSA picks up the waffles and leaves. HILDUR looks
> around helplessly, then takes PRILA's dress and starts
> to sew.*

Midnight Friday.

> *KARI in the cellar. He has been drinking.*

KARI   (*whispers*) Prila? (*He takes a slug from a bottle in his
            pocket. SISSA enters carrying a cup and waffles.*) Sissa.
            Where's your sister?

SISSA   (*hands KARI a cup of red currant wine*) Give me the
            blood of Jesus. (*He does. She then puts a waffle in his
            hand.*) Now I will eat his body. (*He puts it into her
            mouth.*) Now bless me. (*She kneels in front of him.*)

KARI   In the name of Thomas Waller, Bix Beiderbecke, and
            the Madonna–

SISSA   Forgive my father, for he has sinned.

KARI   You're all grown up now.

SISSA   Now I'm free.

KARI   Me too. (*takes out the ticket and shows it to her*) Look.
            A ticket to America.

SISSA   Take me. (*in deep desperation*) PLEASE!!

KARI   I've only got one. Don't tell anyone. Sssh!

> *He leaves, swaying slightly from drink. He goes and waits in the shadows outside the house.*

SISSA   (*in cellar, sings to the girl under the floor*)
Hush my mamma don't you cry
You'll go to the big dance by and by
You'll be wearing a new dress just you see
Made out of the rags in which you buried me

> *PRILA hurries into the cellar.*

PRILA   Oh, Sissa, I'm so sorry I missed your confirmation!

SISSA   That's all right. I'm a woman now.

PRILA   You're not any different, Sissa. It takes more than a confirmation.

SISSA   Oh no, you don't understand. I see things. More than you know. You picked me up and took me to your bed when Mamma put me outside in the field.

PRILA   (*hugs her*) You were my little doll. My very own. I was only seven and I thought you were a gift from the elves.

SISSA   So why don't you like me any more?

PRILA   I do! But you won't grow up. Don't you see, if you won't take care of yourself, I'll never be able to leave!

SISSA   Don't worry, you can leave. Go now. I'll be fine. *Go!* Kari's looking for you.

> *PRILA leaves her. KARI comes out of the shadows and catches hold of her.*

PRILA   Kari!

KARI   Prila. I want you to say yes to Petur.

PRILA   What? I don't understand you–

KARI   I've worked it all out. Come to America in
September–

PRILA   To Boston–?

KARI   I'll be waiting for you in New York.

PRILA   How will you get the money to leave?

KARI   I'll manage. Don't worry. It's the way it was always
meant to be. He doesn't have to know. You don't have
to marry him yet–

PRILA   But I'd have to lie to him–

KARI   Don't think like that. Do you want to spend the rest
of your life with a man who wants to stop you from
singing? This is our chance!

>   *They kiss passionately.*

SISSA   (*in the cellar, speaking to the Hiddenfolk*) You choked my
father to death and put a rock in Mamma's heart, and
I know now. You all came back too late. You never
should have left your baby behind. Go back across
the fiord, and don't ever come back.

>   *The Hiddenfolk sound turns into a strong gust of
wind. The window rattles. Music. SISSA kneels as if
at a grave.*

She's as old as she'll ever be.

>   *SISSA slips away.*

PRILA   (*pulls away in shock*) You're drunk!

KARI   I'm fine, don't worry.

PRILA   You're stinking *drunk*!

KARI   What's this got to do with anything? Prila–!

PRILA   You lied to me.

KARI   (*He grabs her. We see a flash of the mean drunk of the old days.*) Are you coming, or not?

PRILA   (*shakes him off*) I should kick you in the teeth.

KARI   Don't. (*smiles ruefully*) I won't be able to play my horn tonight. Just keep me from falling too far.

        PRILA runs off.

KARI   (*calls after her*) Prila! You'll sing with me tonight, won't you?

        He follows her, but stops as PRILA goes into the house.

HILDUR   (*in the kitchen sewing PRILA's dress, having overheard PRILA and KARI*) Women have a weakness for slippery men.

PRILA   (*furious*) That's enough! Who gave you permission to plan my life for me?

HILDUR   (*throws the dress at PRILA*) There's your dress. I finished it.

        HILDUR leaves. PRILA goes to the switchboard.

PRILA   Hallo! Raven Canyon Radio! Is this Jim Swing? Jim! I have no time for little talk. No! Listen. I will *not* sing tonight at your Big Band Bash unless you give every girl in town silk stockings. *Hundreds.* Take them to the dairy. Yes! *Hurry!*

        PRILA runs off with her dress.

JIM   (*hurries in to Radio Station and speaks on microphone*) Jim Swing here with a mission for the troops! We got an emergency call for silky stockings! Just go on up to the dairy and fill that place with every Icelandic girl's dream! We need *hundreds* of pairs! If you don't get your butts up there now, there may be no gals to dance with! Clean your teeth, shave real close, and shine your shoes! Tonight is the *night*! Oh, and thanks to all the guys who parted with a whole week's supply of precious booze. 200 hundred bottles of beautiful Southern Comfort! A little thank you, to the local guys, for the privilege of dancing with their gals. And guys, be on your best tonight. Mind your manners. See you at the Bash! (*whips out a comb, splashes on cologne*)

Saturday Night.

Outside the Temperance Hall. PETUR stands with a notebook and pencil. JIM arrives.

JIM   Oh Man! (*to PETUR*) Uh, Peter. What are you doing out here? Didn't you guys get the Southern Comfort? (*beat*) D'you need some more?

PRILA arrives with a coat over her Rita Hayworth dress and a scarf over her hair.

Hey Prila!! Did you gals get the uh–? (*indicates stockings*)

PRILA   Yes – thank you.

JIM   (*sees the tension between PRILA and PETUR*) It's OK, Petur. We're just– (*sighs*) good friends – I guess.

PRILA   (*to PETUR*) So you are going to do it?

PETUR   Yes.

PRILA   All alone?

PETUR   You're being watched.

PRILA   By whom?

JIM   What you guys saying?

PETUR   Look up there. The road is lined with men.

PRILA   (*looks up*) How many?

PETUR   Everyone. They found out about your plans for
          the silk stockings. It seems that some *wives* were
          collecting stockings too. The band is waiting to play
          at the hotel. The decorations are up, and the only
          people who showed up were men.

PRILA   So now they've come to see who'll walk through
          these doors?

PETUR   Do you know who will? You seemed to have master-
          minded this!

PRILA   What are you going to do about that?

JIM   You know, it's strange. When you folks are talking
          your language you always sound like you're fighting.

**PETUR &
PRILA**   We *are*!

          *KARI arrives carrying the cornet case. He stops and
          looks at PRILA.*

JIM   Kari! Ready to swing? We should warm up–

PETUR   This town will never forgive you.

KARI   You mean *you*–

PRILA   Kari. The band's waiting.

KARI   Go back to your books little schoolboy. You're not up
          to this.

          *KARI starts to leave. PETUR grabs his arm. He
          shakes it off.*

JIM   Whoa, there, pal!

PETUR   I'm not going anywhere till you make your choice.
          Are you going?

KARI   It's Prila's choice.

PETUR   What do you mean?

KARI   You'll find out in good time.

PETUR   Put down that horn. (*pushes him*)

PRILA   Kari! Go inside, before you–

KARI   (*laughs as JIM laughs amiably along*) You don't fight! You go behind people's backs. That's your style. Couldn't even find yourself a woman of your own. I know all about Nurse Petur! It's not nursing that wakes up a woman.

PETUR   What is it? Carving her face up with broken bottles?

>   *A shocked silence. PRILA steps between them. She hardens visibly.*

PRILA   Jim.

JIM   Uh – yes, Prila?

PRILA   I am sorry that you have to see this display. I will see you inside. We will have fun tonight. You have made many women feel fine under our dresses. (*kisses him flirtatiously and says to KARI and PETUR in English*) Perhaps you can both learn a little of this man's style.

>   *PRILA turns and goes onto the stage with the band.*

JIM   (*swooning*) I am your slave! Uh – sorry Peter! I guess she's the boss.

PETUR   Keep your hands on your drumsticks, soldier.

>   *KARI goes in to the dance hall. SISSA appears. She is wearing the Bette Davis party dress from "Dark Victory" and holding a long cigarette holder. She has on her ruby red slippers.*

JIM   Well hallo Bette Davis! Uh – don't I know you?

SISSA   "Oh, Gerry! Don't let's ask for the moon! We have the stars!" (*She sweeps past them into the dance hall.*)

> *HILDUR enters from up the hill, looking splendid in traditional Icelandic costume.*

PETUR   Hildur!

> *She goes to PETUR.*

HILDUR   You shouldn't have said whores.

PETUR   You're going in there?

HILDUR   In my traditional dress. Your idea. Keep your eyes on the hill. Five hundred Strandvik women are on their way. Even the married ones are coming. See what you started? (*lifts up her skirts to show her legs*) Silk feels good against the skin. Write my name down.

> *As she goes into the dance hall, the music swells. PETUR looks up the hill. Rhythm starts up.*

PETUR   Oh my God!

JIM   What? (*following PETUR's gaze*) Oh *man*! Wow! What a sight!

> *A golden glow from the sky radiates over PETUR and JIM's faces as they look up the hill. At the same time PRILA appears on stage looking ravishing as Rita Hayworth.*

Wow! There's Ginger! And I think – yes it's Katherine Hepburn! I'm in heaven!

> *He runs to the band and starts a drum beat. At the same time, the sun colours the sky with the richest sweep of colour from gold to deep crimson. Against the intense colour the silhouettes of film stars appear, and pause as if caught in a Hollywood film.*

PETUR   What have they done? (*feverishly starts writing the names*)

Inside the Temperance Hall the band is in place. KARI
appears from behind the stage, with cornet and a bottle
of Southern Comfort. He puts the bottle beside his
case. During PRILA's speech he takes a long pull of
the bottle, then gets ready to play cornet.

PRILA   (*enters and speaks over the drum rhythm*) Hallo
American friends! Tonight is the first time ever, that
we have a band with Americans, and Icelanders! Now
get ready for a long night! Nobody goes to bed until
the sun goes down! And it does not set for a month!
(*The crowd roars its approval every time she pauses.*) Hit it
boys! (*sings*)
"What good is melody what good is music
If it ain't possessin' something sweet?
It ain't the melody it ain't the music
There's something else that makes the tune complete
It don't mean a thing if it ain't got that swing
Doo wah do wah do wah do wah do wah do wah do
wah do wah
It don't mean a thing all you gotta do is sing
Doo wah do wah do wah do wah do wah do wah do
wah do wah
It makes no difference if it's sweet or hot
just give that rhythm everything you've got"

During the song SISSA weaves around the periphery
of the main stage action sensuously. HILDUR is also
at the periphery of the band, watching the crowd on
the floor. The song reaches the bridge "It makes no
difference if it's sweet or hot" then suddenly the sound
of crashing glass! Weird shadows appear on the walls.
A fire engine clangs. Sounds of a hundred male voices
roaring and screams of women. Everyone on the stage
scatters. SISSA runs off. PRILA calls out.

PRILA   SISSAAA!!

PRILA runs off. The stage is almost blacked-out,
except for the shadows fighting against the red sky.
KARI stands alone among the shadows. The shadows
are similar to the Hiddenfolk shadows of the opening of
the story, only more malevolent and they seem to be in
battle. As KARI plays, a wind whistles up. He is

drunk. He is the eye of the storm. The sounds are all around, just as loud, but dreamlike.

Behind the dance hall. PRILA comes dragging SISSA. She has SISSA's dress in her hand. SISSA is half-naked and struggling and screaming. She is dead drunk.

SISSA   Let me go!

SISSA tries to run. PRILA drags her back.

PRILA   You're going home! Mamma! I found her!

HILDUR   They can't put the fire out. It's spreading! Let's get out of here.

SISSA   No! I have to go back to him!

PRILA   She was up against the wall with a stinking drunk soldier.

HILDUR   Come on girl! Quickly! Put your clothes on!

SISSA   Go to hell, old woman! You're not my Mamma.

HILDUR   You're right. I'm not. I don't want a slut for a daughter.

SISSA   I'm not a slut. I'm in love!

PRILA   Sissa! Everyone's gone crazy. Do you want the Strandvik men to catch you being screwed by that Americani and shame you in front of the whole town?

SISSA   My soldier will protect me.

PRILA   He's not protecting you. He's *using* you!

SISSA   (*to PRILA*) You don't know what's real! I'm not going to listen to someone like you! You lie to people! You break their hearts! Everybody loves you, and you can't even feel it! No wonder Kari decided to go to America without you!

PRILA   What?

SISSA   He showed me the ticket! He's leaving tomorrow! He planned it all along.

HILDUR   Hah! I *knew* it! What did I tell you? Sucks you in, then dumps you!

PRILA   (to HILDUR) You're happy aren't you?

> *SISSA watches the two women launch into their fight, and slips away unseen.*

HILDUR   I won't stand by and watch my daughter throw herself after a useless man!

PRILA   You don't have any daughters left!

HILDUR   What?

PRILA   You're alone now.

HILDUR   What's going to happen to you?

PRILA   What do *you* care? You've got what you want. A big empty house. No one left to be angry with!

HILDUR   No! Prila – not like this– (*PRILA walks away from her and leaves her alone. HILDUR walks slowly away and goes into her house and sits.*)

> *SISSA rises up in front of the flaming sky with Clark Gable. PRILA is alone at the harbour. The sound of breaking glass continues. The flames of the fire rage against the sky. Army sirens.*

SISSA   Oh Clark Gable! You've come to fly me over the rainbow!

> *PETUR runs on.*

PETUR   Prila! You're safe! I've been looking for you everywhere. I was so afraid you'd been hurt.

PRILA   He's gone.

PETUR   Maybe – things will be all right again–?

> *Clark Gable wraps SISSA up gently in his arms and kisses her. They remain in the embrace at the edge of the cliff, under the red sky.*

PRILA   I was going to follow him–

PETUR   I don't want to hear–

PRILA   –And now your heart is broken. I did that.

> *SISSA falls into Clark Gable's arms. He carries her limp unconscious body away.*
>
> *PETUR and PRILA are alone.*

PETUR   Yesterday, when you asked me what I wanted – I wanted – to – put my arms around you, and tell you I loved you–

PRILA   But you thought you'd look like a fool.

PETUR   I am.

PRILA   So am I.

PETUR   I love you. Will you – marry me–?

PRILA   (*breaking down*) It's the wrong time to ask. (*She leaves.*)

Sunday Morning. Harbour.

> *Wind and rain. Cold. JIM arrives. KARI is lying curled up with his cornet, waiting for the south-bound trawler.*

JIM   Hey, Buddy! Rise and shine.

> *Sees KARI's hangover in all its glory. KARI shakily reaches for his cornet case, opens it and finds the ticket. He puts it in his pocket.*

Man. You look like I feel.

> *KARI finds a bottle of liquor with a few inches of
> liquor left in it. He drinks thirstily.*

You hitching a ride again?

KARI   I have a ticket to your country.

JIM   I sure would like to come with you. Look, could you
– if I give you the address, could you look up my
Mom? She's in Kansas.

KARI   Kansas? There is good music there.

JIM   Oh yeah! That's all you live for, ain't it?

KARI   (*laughs*) Is there anything else?

JIM   You're a *cool cat*. The real thing.

KARI   I hope I am.

JIM   (*writes on a piece of paper*) They'll dig you. Use my
name!

KARI   You are not coming back here?

JIM   Going into action. Just heard this morning. They've
assigned me to the radio room on one of our
destroyers – the *Witchita*. Now that Sergeant Cooper's
arrived, they're putting my new-found talent to use
on the high seas. No more drumming for a while, but
I brought these along anyway. (*pulls his drum sticks out
of his pocket*) Who needs drums?

KARI   Every good band.

JIM   Yeah. Well. It was great playing with you – until those
Icelandic guys attacked the dance hall. Hundreds of
crazy guys out of nowhere, throwing empty Southern
Comfort bottles through the windows. I guess we
shouldn't have sent that truck load of booze to the
other dance. You Icelandic guys! You turn into King
Kong after a few drinks. I must have hit one guy ten
times before he dropped. He went down like a god-
damned tree. Didn't feel a thing. Well, at least the rain

put the fire out, and nobody died. Hey. That Peter guy doesn't like you much does he?

KARI   My brother

JIM   Your *brother*? I guess you're not a happy family.

KARI   Like in the movies? (*laughs*) We were. Once.

JIM   (*pulls out a bottle*) Here.

>*KARI drinks long and hard through the following:*

I've figured out what that midnight sun does to you. It makes you think you're dreaming, and awake at the same time. I've even got to thinking you *people* ain't quite real. Like that Billie kid in the Bette Davis dress, asking everyone to take her to Hollywood. Crazy!

>*Sound of a trawler. SISSA appears. She carries a bag. She stands a little apart from KARI and JIM. She looks hopefully out to sea. Neither of the men sees her.*

>*In HILDUR's kitchen, the telephone exchange starts to buzz. HILDUR pauses then goes over to the board and picks the headphones up. She tentatively plugs in.*

HILDUR   Northern Iceland Telephone. Yes this is Hildur. I am well – thank you. Ah – and you? To whom do you wish – the Dairy? Hold on. Putting you through. (*She sits at the exchange with the headphones on.*)

>*Music starts.*

JIM   Oh boy, I will *never* forget the vision of those women coming to the dance. Looking up the hill, against a cherry-red sky. Hundreds of beautiful dames! Silhouettes against a wall of fire! Those heavenly angels, walking down the dirt road, the hems of their skirts lifting a little in the wind. And lips as red as blood! Every one of them a star! Every one more beautiful than the movies. As good as the swans.

                PRILA appears on the stage. They pick up their instruments.

PRILA   (*sings*) Skylark, have you anything to say to me
Can you tell me where my love can be?
Is there a meadow in the mist
Where someone's waiting to be kissed?

                PETUR enters HILDUR's house with the Morning News.

PETUR   (*reads the front page*) "The men of Strandvik have declared the following women Whores of the Americanis; Katherine Hepburn, Ginger Rogers, Greta Garbo, (*He reads the following names quietly under the next section of the song.*) Barbara Stanwyck, Lana Turner, Alice Faye, Claudette Colbert, Joan Blondell, Mary Astor, Joan Crawford, Norma Shearer, Rosalind Russell, Olivia Dehavilland, Jean Arthur, Madeleine Carroll, Greta Garbo, Eleanor Powell, Anna Neagle, Ruby Keeler, Vivien Leigh, Carole Lombard, Hedy Lamarr, Dorothy Lamour, Jean Harlow, Veronica Lake, Mae West, Joan Fontaine, Irene Dunn,

PRILA   (*sings*)
Skylark have you seen a meadow green with spring
Where my heart can go a wandering
Under the shadows in the mist
And in your lonely flight
Haven't you heard the music in the night
Wonderful music
Faint as a will o' the wisp crazy as a loon
Sad as a gypsy serenading the moon
Oh Skylark, Can you tell me if you see these things
For my heart is riding on your wings
And if you see them anywhere,

PETUR   Judy Garland, Bette Davis, (*looks up to HILDUR*) Rita Hayworth.

PRILA   (*sings*)
Won't you take me there?

                The end.

Bad Boy

words & music by Maja Ardal

Sea Blue Sea

words & music by Maja Ardal

Turn in to the mid night sun and en ter hea ven's door

Sea blue blue sea   Sea blue blue sea

We Were Made For Each Other

words & music by Maja Ardal

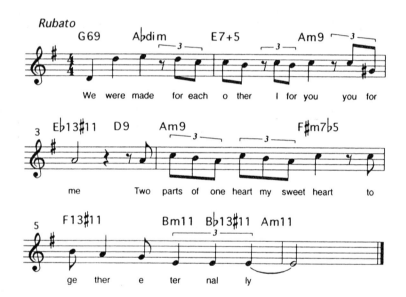

Icelandic Lullaby

traditional translated by Maja Ardal

Hush my ma ma don't you cry   You'll go to the big dance

by and   by You'll be wear ing a new dress just you see   Just

take   off   the   rags   in   which   you   bur   ied   me

Willow Tree

Maja Ardal was born in Siglufjordur in the north of Iceland in 1949. She received her education in Edinburgh Scotland, and studied drama at the Royal Scottish Academy of Music and Drama in Glasgow. She came to Canada in 1970 and acted with Toronto Workshop Productions in 10 plays. She regards George Luscombe as her first mentor. Maja was Artistic Director of Young People's Theatre from 1990 to 1998. A translation of *Midnight Sun* was produced in Akureyri Iceland in the spring of 2001. Maja wrote the book for the musical *Joy* with composer Joey Miller. It was produced at the Workman Theatre in October 2000.

AGMV Marquis

MEMBER OF SCABRINI MEDIA

Quebec, Canada
2001